2019 | Issue #3

U.P. READER

Bringing Upper Michigan Literature to the World

A publication of the
Upper Peninsula Publishers and Authors Association (UPPAA)
Marquette, Michigan

UPPAA

U.P. Reader
Issue #1 is still available!

Michigan's Upper Peninsula is blessed with a treasure chest of writers and poets, all seeking to capture the diverse experiences of Yooper Life. Now U.P. Reader offers a rich collection of their voices that embraces the U.P.'s natural beauty and way of life, along with a few surprises.

The twenty-eight works in this first annual volume take readers on a U.P. Road Trip from the Mackinac Bridge to Menominee. Every page is rich with descriptions of the characters and culture that make the Upper Peninsula worth living in and writing about.

Available in paperback, hardcover, and eBook editions!

ISBN 978-1-61599-336-9

www.UPReader.org

U.P. Reader: Bringing Upper Michigan Literature to the World -- Issue #3
Copyright © 2019 by Upper Peninsula Publishers and Authors Association (UPPAA). All Rights Reserved.

Cover Photo: "Sunset at the St. Helena lighthouse" by Mikel B. Classen. St. Helena Island is an uninhabited 240 acre island in the Lake Michigan about 10 miles west of Mackinac Island.

Learn more about the UPPAA at www.UPPAA.org
Latest news on UP Reader can be found at www.UPReader.org

ISSN: 2572-0961

ISBN 978-1-61599-447-2 paperback
ISBN 978-1-61599-448-9 hardcover
ISBN 978-1-61599-449-6 eBook

Managing Editor - Mikel B. Classen
Associate Editor and Copy Editor - Deborah K. Frontiera
Production Editor - Victor Volkman
Cover Photo - Mikel B. Classen
Interior Layout - Michal Splho

Distributed by Ingram (USA/CAN/AU), Bertram's Books (UK/EU)

Published by
Modern History Press
5145 Pontiac Trail
Ann Arbor, MI 48105

www.ModernHistoryPress.com
info@ModernHistoryPress.com

CONTENTS

The Purloined Pasty

by Larry Buege

Over the weekend, Marquette city police received a two-eleven (robbery in progress) from an irate caller on the northwest corner of Presque Isle. Central Dispatch sent officers Koski and Beaudry to investigate. They discovered Wally Higgenbottom sitting in his deer blind near Sunset Point, his hunting rifle leaning forlornly against the wall of the deer blind. Wally's wife arrived moments later. (She had been listening to the police scanner.)

"I think hunting season ended three weeks ago," Officer Koski suggested. Wally shrugged his shoulders.

"I told him so," his wife replied. "He never listens to me."

Since Wally was not actively hunting when the officers arrived, no citation was issued. That would have generated more paperwork than Koski was willing to tolerate this close to the end of his shift.

"Central Dispatch said you were being robbed." Officer Koski surveyed the spacious deer blind. A six-pack, bag of chips, and a dog-eared copy of an old *Playboy Magazine* rested on a wooden bench. "I don't see anything missing."

"My pasty's missing. The swine stole my pasty. I had it lying here on my bench. I turned my head for a moment and it was gone. I saw the thief drag it out the door."

"Can you describe the perpetrator?" Officer Koski took out his pad to take notes.

"The slimy thief was short—very short. And he had yellow skin."

"Chinese?"

"No, his skin was canary-yellow and covered with red, heart-shaped spots. He had two knobby antennas protruding from his head."

"He's been drinking again," Wally's wife surmised.

"Anything else? Did he say anything?"

"He did blow me a kiss just before he scampered away with my pasty."

A breathalyzer test revealed Wally was on the pleasant side of happy, but not legally drunk. Officer Koski closed his notepad; he had better things to do.

"Looky, looky," Officer Beaudry pointed to a trail of slime leading out the door.

"That's his trail," Wally said. "I told you he was slimy."

Officers Koski and Beaudry followed the trail through the door of the deer blind but quickly lost it in the underbrush.

"We need help," Officer Koski declared. He made a call on his cell phone and twenty minutes later another officer arrived with Kasper the K-9 Kop in tow. The dog handler pushed Kasper's nose into the slime and then turned him loose. Kasper loped off with a howl and disappeared into the woods. When the officers caught up to him, Kasper was vigilantly standing guard over a semicircle of bakery crust—all that remained of a once-proud pasty.

"It was a decent pasty," Wally proclaimed.

"I'm sure the end came quickly," Officer Koski said.

"The pasty felt no pain," Officer Beaudry suggested.

While the officers were consoling Wally, Kasper ate the remaining evidence.

"You do know Wally's been drinking again," his wife said.

"You'll have to come back to the station and fill out a report," Officer Beaudry said, ignoring the wife's comment.

At the station, a police sketch artist drew a picture of the perpetrator from Wally's description. The sketch was compared with a list of known Marquette County felons, but none had canary-yellow skin, with red heart-shaped spots and knobby antennas on his head. Working on a hunch, Officer Koski e-mailed the sketch to Professor Toivo Rantamaki. Rantamaki is the former chair of Paranormal Gastropod Psychology at Finlandia University, and is currently in the depths of the Amazon jungle researching his hypothesis that Amorous Spotted Slugs migrated from the Amazon jungle to the U.P. on a coconut during the Biblical Flood. Professor Rantamaki sent a timely reply confirming that the perpetrator was, indeed, an Amorous Spotted Slug!

"Amorous Spotted Slugs have a weakness for pasties and Mackinac Island fudge," Rantamaki added. "Four husky Amorous Spotted Slugs can easily carry off a pasty." Reaction to the Professor's revelation was immediate and profound. Authorities not only had a description of the thief, they now had a motive.

"We will apprehend this ruthless thief and bring him to justice," proclaimed the police chief. "Larceny of this magnitude will not be tolerated in Marquette. Not on my shift."

"Wally's been drinking again," Wally's wife suggested.

"We cannot judge all Amorous Spotted Slugs by the delinquent behavior of one miscreant A.S.S.," said a spokesperson for *Travel Marquette*. "We are hoping to make Marquette County the Amorous Spotted Slug capital of the U.P. It'll generate millions of tourist dollars."

Slug Lovers In Michigan Empowered released the following statement:

"Those of us at S.L.I.M.E. Headquarters extend our heart-filled sympathy for Mr. Higgenbottom's tragic and senseless loss. Although Amorous Spotted Slugs will occasionally *borrow* a pasty or perhaps some Mackinac fudge, they are lovable and harmless creatures and represent the preeminent virtues of the U.P., which is why we hope to make the Amorous Spotted Slug the official State Slug. The Lower Peninsula has the official State Stone (Petoskey Stone) and the official State Soil (Kalkaska Sand). It is only fitting that the U.P. have the official State Slug. To further our cause, we are asking U.P. residents to report all A.S.S. sightings to our website (www.AmorousSpottedSlug.com)."

The *Marquette Mining Journal* tried to contact Wally Higgenbottom for comment, but he was busy—he was at an AA meeting.

The Amorous Spotted Slug (A Yooper Legend)

by Larry Buege

◆❖◆

Oral history, conveyed through innumerable generations, suggests Amorous Spotted Slugs migrated to Michigan's Upper Peninsula from the depths of the Amazon jungle. According to the local folklore, a primitive tribe of Amorous Spotted Slugs discovered a flyer nailed to the trunk of a jungle palm tree. "Free Ocean Cruise," the flyer boasted. "Animals of All Kinds Welcome." The ship would sail (rain or shine) in thirty days. A gentleman by the name of Noah was organizing the excursion.

By nature, Amorous Spotted Slugs are party animals. So the entire tribe signed up for the cruise and set off on the long trek to the port of departure. After a thirty-day forced march, they had traveled forty-two inches. Then the heavens unleashed a great downpour, and water inundated the low lands and began to cover the earth.

"Help, what shall we do?" one of the slugs cried out.

"We are doomed," replied a unicorn splashing through a nearby puddle, "but you can save yourselves." The unicorn pushed a floating coconut toward the slugs with his horn, and the Amorous Spotted Slugs quickly scampered aboard.

It rained forty days and forty nights, and water covered the land. The Amorous Spotted Slugs crafted a sail from a lily pad, but there was nowhere for the *Coconut Clipper*, as they now called their vessel, to sail. During a particularly violent storm, lightning struck the *Coconut Clipper*, knocking its crew on their posteriors. Fortunately, that segment of the average Amorous Spotted Slug's anatomy is built low to the ground. When they regained consciousness, they began experiencing visions of the future. The electrical charge had altered their brain chemistry, making them clairvoyant.

One such vision suggested the water would part once the days began to wane and the nights became longer. The *Coconut Clipper* would then come to rest in a paradise exceeding their wildest desires. Finally, the days did begin to wane and the nights did become longer, but none of the voyagers was awake to greet the summer solstice. The *Coconut Clipper* jolted to a rest on Presque Isle, (now part of modern-day Marquette, Michigan). The sudden stop awoke one of the Amorous Spotted Slugs. He looked out at the virgin timber and lush green underbrush—this had to be the paradise of their vision.

"Yoo-pee! Yoo-pee!" he yelled to awaken the others. The remaining Amorous Spotted Slugs awoke and looked at the awaiting paradise.

"Yoo-pee! Yoo-pee!" they echoed. The name of the new land stuck and the Amorous Spotted Slugs became the first Yoo-pers.

To commemorate their long voyage, Amorous Spotted Slugs now celebrate the summer solstice (or "Yoo-pee, Yoo-pee" day as they refer to it) with a Thanksgiving Feast of pasties and Mackinac Island fudge. For dessert they serve coconut cream pie in tribute to the Great Coconut that carried them to the Promised Land.

Larry Buege's short stories have received regional and international (English speaking) awards. He has also authored nine novels including the ever-popular *Chogan* Native American series. More information about his novels can be found at www.Gastropod-publishing.com or by contacting the author directly at LSBuege@aol.com. For a tongue in cheek look at the campaign to make the Amorous Spotted Slug our state slug, please visit www.AmorousSpottedSlug.com/

![Arch Rock on Mackinac Island photograph]

Arch Rock on Mackinac Island (1900)

Grand Island for a Grand Time

by Mikel B. Classen

◆❖◆

Trout Bay - west side

M unising Bay is a beautiful and popular destination for travelers who want to see the finest that the Lake Superior basin can provide. Home of Pictured Rocks National Lakeshore, an unusual amount of waterfalls, the United States' only underwater preserve, and the majestic Grand Island, the bay is a rare place indeed. In May of 1990, Grand Island was acquired by the U.S. Forest Service and designated by congress as a National Recreation Area. Now much of the island is in public hands, and between its history and natural beauty, it is worth the small effort it takes to spend some time there.

Grand Island is most times seen from an overlook in Munising, yet a side trip to the island can be a special experience. Williams' Landing on Grand Island is one of the old-

est place names on Lake Superior, and Abraham Williams and his wife were one of the first settlers to brave life on the Lake Superior frontier. The history here shaped life all along the Superior shoreline.

The 13,000 acre Grand Island, just offshore Munising in the bay, complements Pictured Rocks, though it is not a part of the national park. It is a separate entity that is under the control of the U.S. Forest Service and not the National Park Service. Not nearly as famous, it is less known as a destination. This affords a much quieter and personal experience for an individual or a family.

Currently, a visit to the island is very private, and can be an exceptionally rewarding experience. There are established primitive campsites on the south end of the island at Murray and Trout Bays. They are within two miles of where the ferry puts in at Williams' Landing. There are tent sites all around the island, but in the summer months reservations are required. There are a couple of cabins that can be rented. These are reasonably new and are very nice to stay in.

Grand Island is a paradise for silent sports. Hiking, biking, and paddling are all encouraged. Trails crisscross the island, making most places of note accessible. For paddlers, in Murray Bay are two shipwrecks that are in shallow water, visible from the surface. Buoys mark their locations. Grand Island is designated as part of the Lake Superior Water Trail.

One of the trails is a history loop. It meanders through the settlement of Williams' Landing. Many of the original old homes and homesteads still stand. Several are still lived in as private residences, and are not a part of the recreation area. Their privacy should be respected.

Grand Island and Williams' Landing was one of the earliest settlements on Lake Superior. When Lewis Cass led his expedition in 1832, Abraham Williams was already here. The only older inhabited places on Lake Superior are Sault Ste. Marie, and Grand Portage. There once was a small Native American community that lived alongside of them.

Over time, the island evolved into a resort destination. The distinctive barn-shaped Williams Hotel, which is recognizable on the shore, was a destination for the rich and elite. It now is in private hands and can only be viewed from the water.

Because of the island's popularity, a tycoon by the name of Mather decided he would build the ultimate hunting lodge. He purchased a large tract of land on the northwest side of the island and built a magnificent lodge on the shoreline. He then stocked his new hunting lodge with exotic game animals. He had them imported from around the world. Unfortunately many of them couldn't take the severe Lake Superior climate and died. The lodge was a failure. It still stands on the west side of Grand Island, looking out over its own quiet bay.

During prohibition, the north side of the island was used as a dropping place for illegal booze. Caves are carved into the rocks and the bootleggers would leave casks of liquor there. Later, someone from the mainland would come by and pick it up when the coast was clear.

Stone Quarry Cabin

Cemetery

For many years, the island was owned by Cleveland Cliffs Iron (CCI) and then the U.S. Forest Service took it over. Their mandate was to turn it into an interpretive recreation area. They have done just that. Highlighting the natural and the historic, Grand Island is a treat for the senses as well as the imagination. Signs placed throughout the island help interpret and visualize the whole that is Grand Island and its past.

A ferry service runs from the mainland to the island from May to the beginning of October. There is all-day ferry service for both passengers and gear, including bikes and kayaks. You can even rent some from them right there at the ferry. The only vehicles allowed on the island belong to the residents and the U.S. Forest Service. Snowmobiles are allowed in the winter, and ATVs only after October.

The two established campgrounds at Murray and Trout Bays have camping sites, but camping is allowed throughout Grand Island where there are established tent sites. The U.S. Forest Service has made some incredible choices for site locations. Nowhere in the park are you far from a designated campsite. Water sources and pit toilets are also scattered about the island along the trails.

In the winter, Grand Island has become the place of choice for snowmobilers and cross-country skiers. Past winters have seen estimated visitors numbering over 3,000 visiting the unique winter wonderland that the island has to offer. From January through March, the bay is frozen solid and access to the island is safe and simple. Powell Point Landing, which is one mile west of Munising, is the closest access from the mainland, and it is only a half-mile jaunt across to Williams' Landing on Grand Island. From there you are free to travel the seemingly endless miles of trails and roads that provide some of the finest winter fun the U.P. can offer.

Ice climbing has become the new exciting winter sport that is seeing quite a few enthusiasts in the winter. Many of the cliffs seep spring water, and in the frigid months, these freeze into giant ice columns. With the right kind of gear and skills, the sport is exhilarating and is attracting new participants all the time.

Grand Island is like a smaller version of Isle Royale that is a lot closer and easier to get to. It can be enjoyed in a day or as long as your time allows. It is a showplace for nature that displays the variety and beauty that is so prevalent in the Munising area. No matter what time of year, the island lives up to its name. From the immense ice formations that hang from the shoreline cliffs, to the intense fall colors that adorn the mixed hardwood and pine forest, to the lush colors of spring and summer, there is ever changing beauty that will present something different every trip.

Grand Island is a recreation playground that is in a class by itself. The island is accessible to all, and there will be no one who can't enjoy Grand Island in whatever adventure they want. The island is a wonderful experience that few are making use of. At the height of the summer season, there are many campsites available and a day trip to the island either hiking or biking can be a great way to get acquainted with the place. Spending time in this Alger County paradise should be a part of any Munising area trip. Go beyond the overlook and take some time to not just look at the view, but experience it firsthand.

Thunder Cove

Mikel B. Classen has been writing about northern Michigan in newspapers and magazines for over thirty-five years, creating feature articles about the life and culture of Michigan's north country. Currently he is Managing Editor of the *U.P. Reader* and chair of the UPPAA Publications Committee.

Classen makes his home in the oldest city in Michigan, historic Sault Ste. Marie. He is also a collector of out-of-print history books, historical photographs and prints of Upper Michigan. At Northern Michigan University, he studied English, history, journalism and photography. He lives with his wife, Mary L. Underwood, and his Labrador retriever, Gidget.

His books include *Au Sable Point Lighthouse, Beacon on Lake Superior's Shipwreck Coast;*, *Teddy Roosevelt and the Marquette Libel Trial, Lake Superior Tales* and *Journeys into the Macabre.*

To learn more about Mikel B. Classen and to see more of his work, go to his website at www.mikelclassen.com.

Lighthouse in East Channel

#2 Pencils

by Deborah K. Frontiera

Whenever I look at a pencil—especially those plain, yellow, six-sided #2 pencils—school, and therefore teachers, come to mind. Pencils and teachers—they are forever intertwined. My personal favorite pencil was the #4 because the harder lead stayed sharp longer. I detest dull pencils. Since the advent of the standardized tests which require a #2, I'm not even sure if they make #4 anymore. Those fill-in-the-bubble tests made their debut while I was in high school, and we had to take the ACT or SAT for college entrance. There were no prep classes and all the nonsense there is today. Our test prep was to get a good night's sleep and to eat a hearty breakfast on the day of the test, and don't forget—you have to bring *#2 pencils.*

Our teachers simply taught their subject matter. Some of them better than others, of course. Some of them more memorable than others—for better and for worse. So begins this mind ramble about pencils and teachers.

•••

Mrs. T came to my name on her sixth grade class roster, "De-BOR-ah Olson."

Indignant, I responded, "It's DEB-or-ah, preferably Debbie." She glared at me over the top of her reading glasses and down her pointed witch's nose, and called out the next name.

Okay, we both set a bad tone for the first day of the school year, but SHE started it!

Or maybe my four older siblings, who had also had Mrs. T for their sixth grade teacher, set up the bad reputation for our family name. That's a good possibility since another teacher—the high school math teacher whom I would meet in the next year in 7th grade—had this response when he saw my name on the roster, "*Another Olson?!*"

"Don't worry; I'm the last one," was my response that time. Mr. M and I did get along, though, even if I wasn't his top math student—never had much of a sense of mathematical logic.

That lack of mathematic sense was due in a large part to Mrs. T, who taught strictly by rote memorization of the "rules" of adding, subtracting, multiplying and dividing. Mrs. T. probably taught by rote because that was how she had learned. Looking back, she probably didn't understand the basic concepts herself, couldn't explain them, and therefore taught the way she was taught, and God help you if you asked a question she couldn't answer!

I did that—asked questions—a *lot!* I was always asking her questions she couldn't answer. Did I do it on purpose? Yes and no. I was curious. I wanted to know about a lot of things. I'd always been a question-asker, but I don't remember my previous elementary teachers being so bugged by my questions. Maybe I asked simpler questions at those younger ages and my previous teachers could still answer them. But by 6th grade, I was trying mightily to put some logic to this math stuff—and I have a very strange sense of logic.

When we began to work on multiplying and dividing fractions, my sense of logic completely fell apart. "Mrs. T," I asked one day, in my best voice, not wanting to be yelled at—again—but genuinely wanting an explanation, "why is it that when you multiply numbers, you get bigger numbers, but when you multiply fractions, you get smaller fractions?" It really made NO sense to me at all. (Much later in college, I would finally understand that multiplying fractions "thing" when I had a class called "Math for Elementary Teachers" that actually explained the concept and also how to teach it.)

It was silent for maybe a minute. Mrs. T. finally spoke, "Well, because that's the way it is. Multiplying means 'of': two groups OF two are four; and ½ OF ¼ is 1/8."

I was not satisfied. I asked again. Her response was the same, but her tone the second time was clearly irritated. "I still don't understand. Why is the answer smaller?"

Mrs. T's third response was that I should be quiet, listen, pay attention, and let her get on with the lesson. Too bad Mrs. T didn't have all the fancy drawings, charts, pictures and technology available today that would have let me get a clear picture of what she was talking about. But they didn't teach it that way back then.

That year was very uncomfortable for me. Mrs. T made me sit right in front of her desk, her nose always looking down on me condescendingly, like I was nobody and should just keep my mouth shut. Often, she didn't even call on me when my hand was up— even to answer a question, because I'd ask a question before I answered hers.

I hated sixth grade. I soaped her windows thoroughly on the night before Halloween! That was the tradition in the village of Lake Linden where I grew up. October 30th was Fawkes Night. I think it came from an English tradition about some man named Guy Fawkes who snatched something valuable from under the eyes of English military guards, and then actually put it back the next night—or so we were told. There were a lot of "Cousin Jack" English in Lake Lin-den (balancing out the French Canadians) which is probably the reason we had such a "celebration." Now, the actual history behind it had something to do with planting explosives in the Parliament building in England on Nov. 5, 1605—and there was a lot of Catholic/Protestant stuff behind it—you can look it up on the internet if you are interested. For us, Oct. 30/Fawkes Night, had to do with playing tricks on people like rubbing dry soap bars on windowpanes, overturning trash cans, and other such fairly harmless pranks.

I got my revenge on Mrs. T's windows and then I did what I had to do for the rest of the school year and endured Mrs. T. She receives an F on my teacher report card.

•••

Much later in life, when I chose teaching for a career, I realized Mrs. T had taught me an excellent lesson: *Do not be that kind of teacher!*

When I became a kindergarten teacher, I put those "do nots" to use in my own classroom. I embraced my children's crazy senses of logic and guided them through such things without belittling them.

An example: The nickel should be 10 cents and the dime 5 because the nickel is bigger—therefore worth more in a five-year-old's sense of logic.

"I know it doesn't seem to make sense," I would respond. "Yes, it seems that the bigger coin should be worth more, because the quarter is worth the most, but somebody else decided the dime is 10 cents and you just have to remember it. I'm sorry." (Fifty-cent pieces had pretty much disappeared by then, or at least were not introduced in kindergarten.)

Or: "Mommy taught me to print my name with all big letters."

"Yes, and she did a really good job of it, too. You write your name very well. That's the 'home' way you learned and you can keep doing that at home. Now I'm teaching you the 'kindergarten' way to write your name, and we use one big letter and the rest little."

Or the day the two Spanish-speaking children came to me on the playground.

"Se habla Espanol?"

"Mui poco," (Very little—which was a stretch because I could barely count to ten and say the above phrase properly.)

The two of them had obviously been arguing about something. They both started talking at once. I put my hand up to stop one with a gesture and pointed to the other to speak. Number 2 began to interrupt. I said, "No, wait," and continued to point to Number 1. When Number 1 finished, I pointed to Number 2, who took her turn, saying her side. When she finished, I pointed back to the first. Their voices changed and pretty soon the two little girls were hugging each other and ran off to play. I have *no clue* what the argument was about. They just needed a mediator.

I also never put students down for poor grammar. I would simply say a phrase correctly in context several times throughout the day. Sometimes I'd talk about "home talk" and "school talk" without ever making one better or worse, just different.

•••

I never went to visit Mrs. T. once sixth grade was over. But thanks, Mrs. T., your negative teaching style with me had an indirect effect on over 500 children a generation later. Several of them came back over the years to visit me and say thanks and tell me the sweet memories they had of kindergarten. Three years before I "retired," I met one of them again. I was at a multiple-day workshop to prepare to pass a test—to be taken using #2 pencils, of course—for the ESL (English as Second Language) endorsement on my teaching certificate—the sort of an endorsement that would let me continue what I'd already been doing for twenty years, but formally, and "on paper." This young woman looked familiar around the eyes. "Do you remember me, Mrs. Frontiera?" she asked.

"I remember your face, but sorry, not your name."

She had been in my very first kindergarten class in 1985 at Pugh Elementary in Houston Independent School District!

I shall spend less time on a few other teachers who come to mind. Mr. M., mentioned previously, taught almost all the math classes at Lake Linden-Hubbell High School. He had six different preps every day: 7th and 8th grade math, algebra 1, geometry, algebra 2, and "senior math" which was a bit of pre-calculus, statistics and trigonometry. If you were bound for college, you knew you'd have Mr. M for six straight years.

Mr. M gets an A+ for simply putting up with me, especially in geometry and in "proof problems." There could be many "correct" answers in those. If my classmates all solved it with the standard 4-5 steps, I'd gone all around the mulberry bush and had 10-12 steps to come to the same end. Mr. M. was obliged to ask, "Did anyone else have something different?" As I think back, he did tend to roll his eyes when my hand went up. Then the whole class was treated to my crazy sense of logic as I put each of my steps on the chalk board.

Thanks, Mr. M., you taught me to be patient with outside-the-box thinkers.

•••

My kindergarten and first grade teachers get As for loving me. Mrs. McKe. did have to humble me in kindergarten just a little when I tried to take over the class at Thanksgiving time. My older sister had already taught me how to draw a turkey (not the trace-your-hand method) and I was anxious to show off my knowledge. Mrs. McKe. asked me if I'd like to teach the class. Shyness took over at that point. Miss F. in first grade was not the least bit upset when I threw up all over the floor one day. She calmly put her hand on my forehead, said I had a fever and told me to go home. (I'm sure she had the office call my mother when she had a classmate take a note to the office requesting the janitor to mop up my mess.) Those two wonderful ladies demonstrated my destiny.

•••

Mr. McKi (not the same last name as Mrs. McKe.) gets an F for crushing my creativ-

Car Ferry dock in St. Ignace (1940)

ity in my senior year. We had to write the weekly essay—250-500 words—always on an assigned topic—usually a boring one. I had this fantastic idea (thank you Mr. S. for physics) about our lives being like kinetic and potential energy. We would start life like rocks at the top of a hill—all potential, no kinetic energy. As we grew, and rolled down the hill, we used up our potential and gathered kinetic energy. Some people had steep hills, others long, smooth ones. Our lives went along until we reached the bottom and coasted for a while, but when all the potential and kinetic energy was gone, we died. I wrote this essay—a well-organized metaphor with a lot of other points about how we spend our roll down the hill—and turned it in one week, knowing well that it was not the assigned topic. I was looking for some kind of response to my idea. All I got was, "C Off topic." I was mortified.

I thought I'd saved that paper, but have never found it. Maybe I threw it away.

Anyway, I never wrote anything creative for a very long time.

It was a good thing my junior English teacher had already taught me to love poetry and literature. (The picture in my yearbook with the face I remember says Mrs. P., but I thought I remembered something different.) Anyway, the memories of that class, and the fact that Mrs. P. had even let the class choose a book that we would all read, and discuss as a class, helped me live through Mr. McKi the following year.

Oh, the class voted for *To Sir with Love*. I'd nominated *A Man for All Seasons*, but I was out-voted by everybody else to one—me—outside the box as usual. I still read the other book as my own choice in addition to the one the class chose.

Other than that off-topic C, I'd never had anything less than an A on any piece of writing, and by the end of my senior year, I'd won two local essay contests. So it came as a shock when my first college paper, under Mrs. B at Stephens College, I got a C. But Mrs. B's critical comments were so instructive that my second paper for her got a B and the third an A with nothing less than that ever again. I even took an elective class from Mrs. B the following year, tough as she was. Mrs. B. gets an A in my book for her excellent constructive criticism. Thanks, Mrs. B. for teaching me the art of rewriting!

•••

I can't leave out my mother, either, who was so obsessive-compulsive about proper grammar that we had change pot on the dining room table. If, during the course of dinner conversation—a requirement in the Olson household—we spoke a grammatical error, Mom would point it out and charge us a penny to be put in the pot. It was mostly full of I-owe-yous, but I learned more grammar from Mom than I did in school—even in a school that was "back to basics" before that was the trend!

"You *take* your books to school," Mom would say. "You *bring* them home. You *lie* down on a bed; you *lay* your books on the table."

Historical Native Woman at water pool in woods

God help us if we used a double negative or "ain't". That would cost us a dime! A dangling preposition or split infinitive cost a nickel. Mom often commented that the mission of *Star Trek*—to boldly go—was incorrect. (That was a brand new TV series—the original—when I was in high school.)

"It should be to go boldly," Mom insisted. I'm sure she would be terribly upset at the current state of casualness in this nation's grammar.

But, thanks to Mom, I am a very good editor of other people's writing. (I do miss errors in my own, though.) However, I acknowledge the changes in language over time so that now, ending a sentence with for, to, etc. and to boldly go are acceptable.

There were a lot of other teachers, and many pencils over the years. Each affected my life in one way or another. I wish I could still find #4 pencils, though. I hate all the new fancy ones with plastic decorations on them—pretty, but they really mess up a sharpener, and the round ones roll off a desk. I'm also glad I'm no longer filling in those bubbles in this test-crazy world we now live in, and sometimes I wonder if pencils in general will become obsolete in the computer age, even for those standardized tests, which are sometimes now completed on computers, not just graded by them. Will the day come when pencils, like quill pens, exist only in museums?

Deborah K. Frontiera grew up in Michigan's Upper Peninsula. From 1985 through 2008, she taught in Houston public schools, followed by several years in Houston's *Writers In The Schools* program. A "migratory creature," she spends spring, summer, and fall in her beloved U.P., and the dead of winter in Houston, Texas. Three of her books have been honor or award winners. She has published fiction, nonfiction, poetry, and children's books. She edits the newsletter for the Upper Peninsula Publishers and Authors Association. For details about her many books and accomplishments, visit her web site: www.authorsden.com/deborahkfrontiera

The Rolls K'Nardly

by Jan Kellis

Travel is my drug of choice. It's more potent than caffeine and as addictive as heroin without the debilitating side effects. It's mood-altering, unfiltered, legal, and doesn't require a prescription or a clandestine meeting in a dark alley. It's socially acceptable, non-fattening, non-allergenic, and non-hallucinogenic (except during road trips after 36 hours of driving).

Unfortunately, it's also habit-forming.

I've racked up my fair portion of airline miles, but my favorite way to travel is the iconic, all-American, traditional road trip, in which I pilot my second home—a class B motorhome—to a long-dreamed-of destination, with plenty of diversions along the way. I control the schedule, the timing, and where and when I'll stop and view the vistas.

Perhaps my love of road travel began in the 1970s when my dad purchased a fifteen-year-old US Air Force van the shape and size of a UPS truck, and converted it into a motorhome.

He painted the navy exterior a blinding silver so it would reflect the heat rather than collect it, as the original hue had done. He insulated and carpeted the entire interior, and built a dinette in the back that converted into bunk beds to accommodate the four of us—Mom and Dad on the bottom, my sister (still a toddler) on the inside top bunk next to me. He built a kitchen counter with a sink and added cubbies everywhere. He installed a refrigerator and a composting toilet and added a bench seat covered in fake fur—the long white and gray arctic variety—in the front of the van behind the engine.

The engine was next to the driver's seat, nestled inside a metal trapezoidal cabinet, the top of which was just below the billboard-sized windshield. It lacked the power required to propel the van along a highway at an acceptable speed. An eight-cylinder engine simply wouldn't fit into the space, so Dad replaced the straight six engine with a V6 to incrementally increase the power.

I remember the day Dad named the rig. We were cooking along at our top speed of 55 mph on a sunny April morning, threading our way west along US-2 toward the Black Hills of South Dakota when Dad said, "Let's call this thing the *Rolls K'Nardly*."

Mom and I must have looked at him askance, waiting for an explanation or a punchline.

His grin promised a punchline.

"It rolls downhill," he paused, "and it k'nardly roll uphill."

The Rolls K'Nardly it was.

We must've traveled a million miles in that van. We took it on family trips to New Mexico, South Dakota, Minnesota, and around Lake Superior. We also drove it from one end of the UP to the other several times each summer to visit Grandma and Great Grandma in the Copper Country. We even took it to the drive-in theatre and saw the original Star Wars movie, smug in our ability to cook and eat dinner while we watched.

There was no standard heater in the van. It was equipped with a black tube that ran from the engine into the van itself, providing a constant blast of hot air from the hole above the front passenger-side wheel well, pointed directly at the spectators on the front bench seat. We kept a cube of foam rubber, about the size of my head, jammed into the heater hole to reduce the risk of heat stroke during summer trips.

Of course, there was no air conditioning, either. The two front doors slid back to open, and one tiny window on the driver's side was the only one that allowed air to enter. Dad installed a ceiling vent to provide slight relief from the heat.

The undersized engine, unrelenting heat, and lack of air conditioning weren't the only quirks we tolerated. The Rolls K'Nardly also burned through a fan belt every 500 miles or so.

Dad bought fan belts by the case each spring and when I turned nine, he determined I was old enough to learn how to replace them.

The routine ran thus: when the fan belt blew, the driver immediately pulled over and parked with the steering wheel cranked as far left as it would go. We'd allow fifteen minutes or so for the engine to cool off while I changed into my fan belt maintenance outfit (perpetually dirty) and prepared for contortions by cracking my knuckles and rotating my shoulders while my sister giggled and ran around in circles.

Mom would make sandwiches or lemonade while Dad supervised my work. I'd scooch backward behind the front driver's side tire until I could no longer see Dad's feet. I made no sudden moves under there since my first lesson, when my rookie hair toss had greased and scraped my cheekbone. Any nose itches or errant hairs would have to wait until I emerged. From this position, I could snake one hand up into the van's gizzard and pull out the old belt if it hadn't already landed on the road. I'd then install the new one, carefully hooking it around the uppermost wheel before stretching it around the lower one. Dad would crouch down and hunch over, reluctant to touch the ground with anything but the toes of his shoes, and peer up into the dim engine cavity.

"Good job," he'd pronounce, and I'd shimmy out from beneath, back into the daylight and away from the odor of hot engine grease. I'd wash my hands and arms and change back into my regular clothes for the next 500 miles, when we'd do it all again.

There were no seat belts in the Rolls K'Nardly, so my sister rode on Mom's lap most of the time. She kept Mom busy with games of patty cake and frequent escape attempts, and I was appointed Chief Naviga-

tor. Dad would give me a general direction, such as "aim us toward Tulsa" and I'd open the tattered, spiral bound Rand McNally atlas and compare our location with the new target. We avoided Interstates because we couldn't keep up with the flow of traffic, but we still wanted a fairly direct route. I'd keep one finger on the map, calling out directions as we rolled onward, and I always wondered how people in geographically generic places such as Kansas or Nebraska identified their homeland. Michigan is the only state that lends itself to easy illustration by holding one's hands a certain way, and I've always found comfort and reassurance in being able to identify my origin by pointing at my own hand. This method of reference is used more often than you might think, especially when I encounter people along my travels from less geographically distinctive states.

My current rig, a 2018 Dynamax, doesn't eat fan belts like light afternoon snacks. It can cruise at a respectable speed on the Interstate and it has air conditioning, a separate bedroom, an onboard generator, and a roomy shower. Oh, and there's no fake fur.

I've traveled thousands of miles in it already, navigating by atlas and GPS, all over Michigan and Wisconsin, through New England to the Maritimes, to Florida, and as far west as Kansas City. It's a stylish ride, but it lacks a certain pizzazz.

Sometimes I feel the ghosts of my parents riding shotgun, watching the world blur past, and for a moment I miss the Rolls K'Nardly and its trail of fan belt crumbs.

Jan Stafford Kellis has written seven books, including the *Bookworms Anonymous* series, *Superior Sacrifices*, and *The Sunshine Room*. She lives in the eastern end of the UP where the inspiration is plentiful. When she's not reading or writing, she's probably visiting her daughters or her sister, or quilting, knitting, traveling, marathon shopping, or luxury camping. She hasn't been bored since 1974, when she first learned how to read. Visit her online at http://JanKellis.com

Seeds of Change

by Amy Klco

Jonathan MacIntosh Jr. went to sleep with a vague sense of hopelessness. This was not a new feeling for him, unfortunately, although Jonathan felt like it should be. After all, wasn't he living the American Dream? He had a very lucrative job in IT. He owned a display-worthy home in the richest subdivision of his city. In addition to a 4-wheel-drive truck, he also owned a motorcycle, a 4-wheeler, and a speedboat. He didn't have the wife and 2.5 children yet, but he figured that was only a matter of time. Why, then, did he feel like his life had no meaning?

When he woke up the next morning, however, he felt something almost entirely new—hope. Excitement, even.

It took him a while to place where the feeling had come from: not from his phone alarm, which he quickly silenced with a swipe of his hand, not from the darkness outside his window, and definitely not from the workday he knew was looming before him. And yet, excitement was in him, all the same.

The dream, he realized suddenly. This feeling of joy came from the dream he'd had. But what had it been about?

Ever so slowly, he was able to pull the events of the dream back into his mind. He was wandering the countryside, going from one small town to the next, with nothing but a rucksack on his back and, was that a stewpot on his head? At each town where he stopped, he left a gift. Seeds. Apple seeds.

Jonathan thought back to the stories he heard in elementary school about Johnny Appleseed. It stuck in his mind because of how the kids picked on him for weeks after that, calling him Johnny (how he hated that name!) and asking him if he had any seeds to share. Even now, the memory of that time filled Jonathan with anger. He was not some weirdo who traveled the country giving away seeds to everyone he saw.

Why, then, Jonathan wondered, did this dream fill him with hope and excitement?

He thought back to the dream again, trying to pull out something that would explain this hopeful feeling. Maybe it wasn't the seeds, he thought. Maybe it was the travel. Maybe his subconscious mind was telling him he needed to go on a road trip. Visit the finest resorts the country had to offer. Maybe then he would be happy.

"Yes, and no, and yes," a part of his mind replied instantly, simply.

He closed his eyes again, trying to bring back the vision. He took three deep breaths. And there he was again, in his mind's eye. Rucksack on his back, cooking pot on his head. But when he glanced down at his hands, he was no longer holding apple seeds. Instead, he held a small plastic object, about the size of a hockey puck, but a little bit taller. Around the edge were various holes, just the right size for: a USB cable, a power cord, an Ethernet cable. It was, Jonathan knew instantly, a wireless internet router—but unlike one he had ever seen before, unlike any that were currently in existence. It was the one, Jonathan realized with a shock, that he would invent,

Kitch iti Kipi Big Springs in Manistique (1949)

one that could pick up wireless signals ten times further away than anything currently available. One that, he realized with a flash of insight, could bring the internet to remote locations throughout the country—throughout the world, in fact.

Jonathan's eyes popped open with a start. "Imagine the money I can make on this," he said aloud to his empty room. "I'll be rich!"

"No," that voice inside him said again. It wasn't angry, it wasn't forceful. Just calm, quiet, yet full of authority. "You will not make a dime on your invention. In fact, you will end up sacrificing almost everything you have in order to share this invention with the world. You will, however, be happy."

There was no point, Jonathan knew, in trying to argue with the voice. This voice was not giving him a suggestion, a possible outcome. It spoke the truth, and Jonathan knew, then and there, that what it said would come to pass.

He called into work that day and sat down right away to sketch the plans for this new router. He had already wasted so much of his life. He had no more time to lose.

"Tell me the story again, Mom," the little boy begged as he was being tucked into bed.

"Once upon a time," she began, "A man had a vision—a vision that would save our world. What seemed like a simple device—an internet router that could be used anywhere in the world—was really the start of a global change in how we all lived. People could leave the big, overcrowded cities, without losing what the cities had to offer. And they did. People migrated to the country. They got in touch with nature again and learned to love her and care for her once more."

"And he just gave these routers away!" the boy chimed in, too excited to wait for that part of the story.

His mother smiled. "Yes, he did," she said. "He sold everything he owned, except for his truck, and traveled all over the country, and then the world, handing out these routers to anyone who wanted them. The only payment he would take for himself was food and shelter for the night."

"But people gave, anyway, didn't they?"

Again, the boy's mom nodded. "Many did. They gave to his foundation, to cover the cost of making more routers, and to invest in new discoveries. It changed the whole way our economy worked and the way we viewed money."

"And what was his name again?" the boy asked, clearly already knowing the answer.

"He was named Jonathan MacIntosh, Jr. But he was better known as Johnny Apple Seed.

The Lovers, the Dreamers, and Me

by Amy Klco

"Adventurers wanted," the sign said. "Join us on the moon colony. All are welcome. Make history! Get a fresh start! Guaranteed living income for all settlers! No work required. Go to www.mooncolony.com for more information."

When Sara read the sign, her heart leapt in her chest. Especially at the last part—"guaranteed living income." Or, as her mind automatically translated, "freedom."

She blinked her eyes twice in rapid session, in order to tell her augmented contacts to take a picture of the flyer. She would download the picture at home and show it to Jack—if she had the nerve. Although she had a feeling she already knew what his response would be, she had to ask. After all, his response would decide everything.

Then she hurried to finish her walk and get back to the apartment in time to serve Jack his dinner when he got home from work, just as she had done every night for the last thirty-three years.

She hadn't been cooking just for Jack all those years, of course. There had been the kids—two boys and a girl. They had had to fight for permission to have the third child. Two was the set limit on kids. But Sara had wanted a girl after two boys. She was willing to fight for permission to have one, promising, among other things, to never work outside the home until the kids were all grown and gone.

Jack's job as the Senior Operations Consultant for CEI Technologies afforded them a very comfortable life, so there was no need for Sara to work, anyway. Plus, Jack enjoyed having her wait on him when he got home every day. So Sara got the girl she wanted and Jack got the wife he wanted and everyone was happy.

But now that the kids were all out of the house, living their own lives, Sara found herself longing for something more. What that something more was, she didn't know. That is, until earlier that day, when she'd read the sign in the Community Gardens, where she always went for her walk. She didn't know what adventures awaited her on the moon, but she knew all too well what she'd be leaving behind.

"So I saw something today," Sara told Jack, as the meal was winding down, after she knew for sure he'd had enough to eat and would be willing to at least listen to her. Then she handed him a printout of the picture she had taken earlier, every detail of the sign captured flawlessly.

Jack read it in silence and grunted. "Ha! Looks like the government is getting desperate to populate that old moon-base. Must be no one wants to go there—they have to bribe people to get them to even consider it."

"It's not a bribe," Sara tried to clarify. "It's just a guaranteed base income. Enough so people don't have to worry. If they can't find a job, they'll still know they are safe, that they can feed themselves and have a roof over their heads."

"Yeah, exactly!" Jack said. "And do you know what kind of people they're going to get with this 'guaranteed living income'? Lazy ones, that's who. People who aren't willing to work and make a life for themselves, that's who. The kind who just want things handed to them."

Jack had always prided himself on being a "self-made man." He had worked hard to get where he was in the company, often working sixty to eighty hours a week. He had missed seeing his boys' basketball games—every one of them. He had never once been to his daughter's violin recitals. Even now, when he could see the boys playing for the NBA on demand whenever he wanted, or watch one of his daughter's internationally broadcast concerts with the click of a button, he didn't have time to bother with such things. His job had afforded them many things in life—including private coaches to help their children become so successful. What his job did not provide for him was the time to appreciate it.

"I want to go," Sara told her husband, almost in a whisper.

"You what?" Jack looked at her like she was from another planet. "Why would we want to leave everything we have to go to some god-forsaken ball of dust?"

"It's not just dust up there, not any more. You know the government has been working hard to terraform it. They have gardens up there and trees and rivers and grass and everything, just like here on Earth. Better than on Earth, they say, since they don't have the pollution we're dealing with."

"That's not the point, Sara," Jack scowled angrily. "The real question is, why would you want to leave everything we have here?"

That was the one question that Sara could not answer. Not to Jack. Not after all he'd done to support the family for so long. Not after she had let him support her for so long.

The truth was simple, and yet impossible to say. She didn't love Jack. She hadn't loved him for years and years, if she'd ever loved him at all. He gave her security. He allowed her to raise her children comfortably. If it weren't for Jack and all his hard work, she would have never been given the chance to have a third child. And Sara couldn't imagine her life—or the world—without her daughter in it. For all of these things, she would be eternally grateful. But that didn't erase this one basic fact—she did not love him. In fact, on nights when she was feeling particularly honest with herself, she had to admit that she didn't even like him all that much.

Unable to say all that to the man she owed her entire adult life to, she simply sat there in silence.

"Well," Jack said at last, "You can forget this foolish nonsense now, because I'm not going anywhere."

"I didn't expect you to go," Sara replied quietly, calmly. "I'm going alone." She was surprised at herself for saying that, and just as surprised at how calm she felt. But there was no need to get upset, no need to argue. This wasn't something to fight about. It was just a simple fact. Jack would stay here, in the world he loved, doing what he loved—working all the time. But Sara was leaving—at last.

It took a moment before Jack said anything, as if his mind had been stopped in its tracks by something so unexpected, something so unknown, he couldn't quite process it. Sara didn't blame him—she had never once given him any reason to suspect that she wasn't happy where she was. No wonder this idea was hard to grasp.

Finally, Jack spoke again. "Oh no, you don't," he told her forcefully. "I don't know who you've been talking to who put this fool notion into you head, but you can forget it now. You are not going to the moon. You are staying right here with me where you belong."

"No, I'm not," Sara replied calmly, surprising herself yet again. She had never disagreed with Jack, not in all their time together. Even during the struggle to get permission to have their daughter, if Jack had told her to stop, she would have in a heartbeat. But this, this was different. This time, she had a way out. And she was going to take it.

•••

A week later, she found herself walking to the Moon Life complex with a small suitcase containing all she cared about in the world. She could have brought more—some people had brought truck-loads full of things, she noticed, watching them unpack. But when it came time for Sara to pack, she found there wasn't much she wanted to keep. All she owned really belonged to Jack—he had bought it for her. And to be honest, most of it wasn't even what she'd really wanted in the first place. But she did bring her laptop. The moon colony, she had been told, was within range of Earth's satellites. She could still holochat with her children whenever she wanted. As far as they were concerned, it would be as if she never left. If, that is, they could ever forgive her for leaving their dad.

Sara sat down on a nearby bench, just watching the other people preparing for the trip of their life. She felt a bit out of place with her one suitcase and no real plans for her future. She knew what she was leaving behind, but really, did she have any idea what she wanted to do once she got to her destination? She didn't have to work—the guaranteed living income would take care of her living expenses. But did she want to work? And if so, what would she do? What did she really know how to do, other than run a household? Perhaps, she thought, this whole idea was foolish. Maybe she should turn around right now, before it was too late, and beg Jack to take her back. He might—if only to save face. But was that what she really wanted?

"Of course not!" she replied aloud to herself, as if she needed to hear her own answer. "I'm not giving up now!"

"Good for you!" replied a young woman, as she sat down next to Sara. "Don't give up now—our adventure is only just beginning."

Sara blushed, embarrassed to be caught talking to herself. She never did that—well, at least not in public. When she had been home, alone, for days on end, well... that was different. Sometimes, she just had to hear a voice, any voice, or she would go crazy.

"My name's Jenny," the younger woman told her, smiling. "And if you don't mind, I would love to hear your story. And document it, if you're willing," she added. She had one of those tablets that records what you said and instantly translated it into print—the kind reporters had been using for years.

"How do you know I have a story?" Sara asked in return.

Jenny smiled sincerely. "Everyone going on this trip has a story. As for me, I intend to interview every one of the 285 passengers. Now. And then again, maybe a year or so from now, to see where they are, to see if this adventure has been all they dreamed it would be."

"Is that your story, then?" Sara asked, easily deflecting the question of her own reason for being there. "Are you a reporter?"

Jenny laughed. "Well, I wasn't. I was a shoe salesperson. But that was yesterday, in my old life. Now, everything can change. Now, I can be whatever I want to be—just like all of us can. No more being held down by a job we don't want to make money to pay bills for things we don't need. Yes," she replied after a moment, "I am a reporter now. I will write down everyone's stories. I will share them with the world. I will explore how this opportunity has made us all free to be who we really want to be. And I'll see how having that chance will affect people. Will they thrive with the freedom to follow their passions? Or will the freedom be too much for them? Will they fall back into their old role because the familiar feels safer? I will see. I will tell the world."

Sara smiled at the young woman, at her face all lit up with passion. She didn't know if everyone on this trip would thrive with their new freedom, but she had no doubt that Jenny would.

"You will, of course, keep our identities secret, won't you?" Sara asked, suddenly worried. She might not love Jack, but she also didn't want to hurt him or make him look bad to his co-workers.

"Naturally," Jenny replied with another smile.

"What stories have you heard so far?" Sara asked, continuing to deflect the question of her own story. She wasn't sure she was willing to share it yet. She wasn't even sure she wanted to think about it too much yet, to be honest. "My husband...I mean, my ex-husband, Jack, said that everyone who is going just wants the free money because they are lazy and don't want to work."

Jenny's happy countenance darkened for a moment. "Yeah, I've heard that a lot—from people who aren't going. Maybe it's their way to try to justify their own cowardliness. It's not easy to pack up everything you own and start over on a new planet." Jenny shrugged. "So far, out of everybody I've talked to, I have found two things in common. The first is they all have a story, a reason for making this trip. The second thing is that they are all brave. And there's not a single one I've meet so far that I would consider lazy."

Sara sat for a while in silence, thinking. Did she fall into the category of being brave? She didn't feel brave—she felt more scared then she'd been in all her life. And yet, she had to admit that it had taken bravery for her to get this far. Telling Jack she was leaving was probably the bravest thing she'd ever done.

"See that couple over there?" Jenny said, pointing to a young couple who seemed to be deeply engrossed in staring into each other's eyes. "They are running away to the moon to elope. They're just hoping their parents don't figure out where they are until after the rocket takes off."

Sara smiled. "Some things never change, do they?" she asked.

Jenny smiled back and nodded. "And there," Jenny added, pointing to another young man, "is the preacher who's going to perform the ceremony, though he doesn't know it, yet. He's going to set up his own parish, one where he can preach the Good Word as he understands it, not just how he's been told to."

Jenny was on a roll. "He's a painter," she said, pointing to a middle-aged man who looked more to Sara like a plumber—but who was she to judge, she reminded herself. "That one fixes antique watches," she added, pointing to another.

"What about the woman over there," Sara asked. "The one who looks like a model?"

"Oh, her? Well, she is a model. She was a model on earth and plans to stay one on the moon. But," Jenny continued with a twinkle in her eye, "She also plans to eat on the moon. As much as her heart desires. She's tired of being told that models have to be paper thin, and she wants to challenge that bias. The nice thing about going to the moon is, even if nobody is willing to pay for her pictures, it doesn't matter. She'll still pose for them all the same—she doesn't need the money to survive. And he's the one," Jenny added, pointing to a small, unassuming man behind her that Sara hadn't even noticed before, "he's the one who's going to take her pictures." Jenny looked at them and smiled. "He's in love with her, you see. He's tried to convince her of it for

years, but she doesn't believe him. She can't believe that he is really in love with her, and not just her body. We'll see what an extra 10 moon-pounds will do for them both."

Sara laughed, imagining the model with an extra 60 Earth-pounds. She would probably look better that way, Sara decided.

Yes, she thought, everyone has a story, a dream that they hope to reach by leaving this planet behind. All of them, except herself. She knew what she was leaving, but...

"I don't know what I'm going to do once I'm there," Sara confessed to this bright young woman. "I guess I'm just coming for the guaranteed living income. Is that bad?"

Jenny looked at her with a twinkle in her eye. "Are you my first lazy person?" she asked, jokingly.

Sara blushed, suddenly embarrassed. "Oh, no. It's not that I don't want to work. I do. I just don't know what I'm going to do. I mean, I haven't had a job outside the home in over thirty years. I don't even know what I could do."

"Well," Jenny replied, suddenly acting very businesslike. "I happen to be looking for an assistant to help with my project. As I said, there are 285 people making this move to the moon colony. And I want to interview every one, both kids and adults. Now and later, to see how their plans turned out. That's a lot of interviews, a lot of information I will need to collect and sort through. I could use some help. So tell me, Sara," she added in formal tone, "what qualifications can you bring to this job?"

"I don't...I mean, I..." Sara stumbled for an answer.

"Do you have a good command of the English language?" Jenny asked.

"Yes."

"Are you task oriented?"

"Of course," Sara replied, thinking of the million tasks it took to run a household.

"Are you good at organizing events? Making schedules and seeing that events run smoothly?"

Again, Sara thought about running a household and nodded.

"As for the last question," Jenny continued, "I don't even have to ask. Are you good at making people feel comfortable enough to talk to you? I already know that's a yes," she said with a wink. "So there it is. The job's yours—if you want it."

Sara sat there for a moment, trying to process what just happened. Had she just had an interview? Had she been offered a job? She hadn't even left for the moon yet...

"I can't offer to pay you much," Jenny confessed. "But then, I get the feeling you're not concerned about the money." Jenny laughed then, a big, hearty, belly-laugh. "Isn't that a good feeling?" she continued. "To be able to make a decision about your life based on what you really want to do instead of on what you have to do to survive. I think I'm going to love it on the moon."

"Me, too," Sara agreed. "And yes, I would love to work for you."

"Not *for* me," Jenny corrected. "With me."

•••

The next year of Sara's life seemed to fly by, almost faster than the rocket that had taken them to the moon. Sara was busier than she had ever been in her life—but happier, too, between scheduling the interviews and hosting events to get the settlers together, Jenny and Sara comparing their versions of everyone's stories, discussing which parts to include in the final book they were writing about the journey, and even how to word it. Sara discovered that she had a knack for writing, and Jenny, being much more interested in interviewing the settlers than in the nitty-gritty of writing the stories down, let Sara do most of it. So Jenny did become the reporter, after all, doing the majority of the interviews. And Sara became the writer she never knew she was meant to be.

As for the settlers' stories, well, some of them turned out well, and others, not so well. The young couple that had eloped were now getting a divorce. She wanted to stay on the moon; he was planning on leaving on the first rocket heading back to Earth. The painter had made 365 new paintings, one a day for a year. Nobody could claim that he was the next Rembrandt—in fact, nobody even wanted to buy any of his paint-

ings. But he was happy doing them and that was what really mattered. The model and her photographer were getting married on the one-year anniversary of their arrival on the moon, the day the rocket would be coming with a load of new settlers, as well as to take back anyone who wanted to return to Earth. Some were going home. Others felt that they were already home here on the moon.

Actually, the model and photographer weren't the only ones getting married on this auspicious day. Sara and Jenny had discovered that, not only did they enjoy working together, they loved just being together. On a world where they could be whatever they wanted to be, they discovered that what they really wanted to be was together—forever.

Sara thought she couldn't be any more surprised. Who would have ever suspected, just over a year ago, that she would leave her husband, move to the moon, become a writer, and meet her future wife.

But fate had one more trick up its sleeve— a passenger on the rocket that Sara would never have expected—her daughter. She had come up to play her violin for her mom's wedding ceremony. And to live on the moon and do what she loved, without having to ever worry again if what she loved provided her enough money to survive.

In olden-times, people used to make wishes upon the stars. But, as if turned out, it wasn't the stars that granted wishes. Instead, the dreams of their hearts finally came true on the moon.

Amy Klco is a teacher, writer, speaker, and owner of the publishing company, Enchantment Press. Her novel *YANA: You Are Not Alone*, is about a teenage boy who is struggling with bullying and depression and the teacher who reaches out to help him. She has a series of four young adult fantasy novels coming out this summer: *Mystic Summer*, *Mystic Fall*, *Mystic Winter*, and *Mystic Spring*. You can find out more about these books and others offered by Enchantment Press at www.EnchantmentPress.com.

The Best Trout I Never Ate

by David Lehto

The little creek talked to me as I made my way along its banks, like a happy baby who can't speak yet, but can gurgle pleasantries. It trickled its way through forest and fields behind my grandmother's house, in Nisula, a small Finnish community on Michigan's Keweenaw Peninsula. In hot summers it would dry up and I would wonder if the brook trout made it down stream to bigger waters. It was a small creek that fed into larger streams that eventually flowed into Lake Superior. My four brothers and I, ages five to thirteen, spent our summers there. We were industrious little Finns, building dams, bridges and forts from scavenged lumber, and splashing around for trout; those beautiful, speckled, fast, intelligent, elusive, delicious trout.

We had never caught one. Our fishing skills, and our equipment, were almost non-existent. We were like cavemen, or cave boys, pounding the creek with sticks. The trout considered us a serious nuisance, a band of gypsy children who barged in every summer to vandalize their little paradise. By the end of August, I'm not sure who was happier to see us leave, my grandmother or the trout. What that poor woman ever did to deserve us, I don't know, but that's how the cards were dealt. We were a pack of wild animals, destroying everything we touched. Still, she'd treat us with compassion, taking us for rides in her old pickup truck, exploring ghost towns and mining ruins, seeing a black bear cross the road in front of the headlights. Once we saw a cougar, with its long tail, run across the road fifty feet in front of us.

She taught us how to find the North Star at night by first locating the big dipper, then following its pointer stars. After a long, exhausting week she'd heat up the sauna for our Saturday evening bath; we were five stinky boys sweating out a week's worth of hot summer dirt. She's gone now. It's too late to tell her how I loved her.

But, let's back up to mid-July on my brother Karl's birthday, when the universe was not quite in alignment. Our adult uncle saw fit to give a fishing pole, a box of sharp hooks and tackle to a nine-year-old boy, who barely knew which end of his rod to hold. Being too smart and too impatient to wait around for instructions, we grabbed the new equipment and scrambled for the creek. Making all the noise that five boys make, you'd think we scared all the trout away. But maybe there was a deaf trout lumbering about, too senile to scurry downstream.

The Upper Peninsula is a mystical place; strange things happen. Once, I awoke late at night to see a wolf-like creature cross the foot of my bed and climb out the window. Maybe I was dreaming, or maybe the drunk down the road had stumbled into the wrong house. Anyway, back to the fishing story. A Rapala is a lure used in open waters to catch large fish like pike, bass and muskellunge. The first thing it caught was my brother's attention. Being big and shiny, he figured the trout would go after it the same way he did. The first miracle happened when he man-

Marquette lower harbor (1863)

aged to tie it to the line without getting any barbed hooks embedded in his fingers. Then, he whipped the rod back, barely missing tree branches and several brothers.

Plunk. The lure landed in the middle of the creek, over a deep pool, near a log jam. What happened next I still can't explain, though I can picture it, vividly, after all these years. A beautiful, twelve-inch, speckled brook trout rose out of the depths, struck the lure, and became hopelessly hooked. He had to be the hungriest, stupidest trout in all of Michigan, possibly the entire country. From the banks of the creek, we erupted with shouts and applause. Hero would be too mild of a word to describe Karl at that moment. It was show off time for the nine-year old fishing champion, the instant celebrity. He started to reel him in, then released the tension.

"I think I'll give him a little slack," he said, "wear him down, tire him out," and several other phrases he'd heard his uncle say. The trout, which weighed all of twelve ounces, had no choice in the matter. Think of Hemingway's Old Man and the Sea, but make the fish small and the man big. Finally, the show wound down, and we headed back to Grandma's with the trophy catch. She was surprised, as were all of us, at my brother's luck. Being a country girl, with some knowledge of trout fishing, she was

even more surprised when Karl showed her the lure he'd caught it on. We watched as she expertly cleaned the fish, put it on a plate, and set it in the refrigerator.

"That'll be Karl's breakfast tomorrow," she said. "I'll fry it up in butter."

Every few minutes one of us would open the fridge and marvel at the miracle trout, until Grandma drove us out with the threat of padlocking the refrigerator door. We went back to the creek to see if any more trout wanted to volunteer for dinner, but on his first cast Karl snagged the lure deep in the log jam. It's probably still there today.

That night I dreamt of fishing tournaments, of reeling in giant trout as crowds cheered from the river bank, of being showered with prizes and kissed by pretty girls. Trout began to swim through my bloodstream, and have ever since.

In the morning, I awoke and rushed down stairs as though it were Christmas. The rest of the boys were already up, and the frying pan was spattering away. We crowded around my grandmother as she put the trout on a plate with some tartar sauce and set it on the table for Karl. Ignoring our bowls of cornflakes, we gazed in wonder as Karl dined on his delicious prize.

I didn't get to taste it, but it was, and still remains, the best trout I never ate.

Pirates, Gypsies and Lumberjacks

by David Lehto

When you don't want to be on a boat anymore, you can't just walk home. Lake Superior pounded that lesson into me, as a young boy, many summers ago.

Our family: five boys, ages six to fourteen, two parents and a dachshund, spent our summers at my grandfather's *Camp* on Keweenaw Bay, about ten miles north of Baraga, Michigan. The *Camp* was a cedar log cabin built by my grandfather in the 1920s. The logs were carved and notched to sit tightly on top of each other with no chinking. "Full scribe," my grandfather called it. The sauna and several outbuildings were built with similar Finnish craftsmanship.

The same way young children are magically pulled to the dangers of a passing train, my brothers and I were drawn to Lake Superior's chilling swells and riptides. Often, we played in the surf until our lips turned purple, oblivious to the immediate dangers.

It was a different era, the 1960s. We didn't wear helmets when we rode bikes. If we slipped and fell, it wasn't someone else's fault. It was up to us to keep our shit together.

"Go ahead and play in the street," Dad once yelled at me. "I've got four more just like you."

Long before smart phones and video games, we played outside. Karl, ten, and Will, eight, were building a "jet engine" from old car parts. Junk was strewn everywhere. By the end of August, we spent an entire day hauling everything to the dump. Frankie,

six, just wanted to hang out with the "big guys." Jack, fourteen, and I cobbled together rafts from logs and scavenged lumber. We didn't have money to buy materials. If you lived within walking distance of the *Camp*, you unknowingly donated a few boards. Check the backside of your garage. I imagined I'd raft off to find Pocahontas bathing on some distant shore, same age as me, eleven. We'd sail away in search of treasure and adventure. I figured she looked something like that girl on the *Land-o-Lakes* butter carton.

There was no phone or television at the *Camp*. There was a radio that gave a primitive weather report, if we ever listened to it. Mostly, we just glanced at the sky. There was no indoor plumbing. We fetched buckets of water from a hand-pump well. But not all chores seemed like work to a child. To get the water to come out, we'd yank on the pump handle like a bunch of jack-happy baboons.

In the summer of '65, Dad acquired the perfect raft, a used pontoon boat. He "horse traded" it from a local farmer for a chainsaw and some advice on how to build a sauna. Owning a tree service and logging business, he always had chainsaws in the back of his truck. He seemed to use them as currency.

The boat needed a lot of work. Along with my older brother, Jack, Dad took the engine apart, poked out the rat's nests, and soon had it purring. My contribution was a bubble-compass I took off the dashboard of a '52 Buick, found while climbing through cars at the junkyard. I mounted it next to the steering wheel. At eleven years old, I couldn't start it, but Dad could yank it like he was start-ing a lawn mower. The big, old motor belched two-stroke exhaust as we chugged up and down the shoreline.

Dad was a reckless boat driver. He'd scrape over submerged boulders, run into floating logs, then ram it up on the sandstone beach. For a guy who wasn't drunk, he could sure wreck a boat.

"Who cares?" he'd say. "All I want is a few seasons of fun."

My brothers and I were ecstatic. Even when it was beached we played on it, attaching ropes and blankets and building forts. We wanted to put our sleeping bags on it and camp out, but Mom said "No." She didn't feel the same as we did. She thought it was dan-gerous. When we decided to take it across Keweenaw Bay to explore the ghost town of Pequaming, she objected.

"I'm going to lose my entire family in one sinking," she exclaimed.

Dad explained that each pontoon was a sealed, airtight chamber, unable to sink. "I'm not impressed with your facts and fig-ures," she responded. "The way you ram it into boulders. If there's a way to sink it, you'll find it."

But Dad had the final say. To us, he was indestructible. We'd gladly follow him into the depths of hell and back.

It didn't matter if you were a drunk lum-berjack or a hungry black bear, when Dad was in work mode, you'd better find your place. But when he was playing, it was al-ways an adventure. We explored old mining ruins, haunted farm houses, or climbed on a stack of cars at the junkyard.

When Mom saw that she couldn't stop us, she reluctantly packed a picnic basket. At the last minute, as we were shoving off, Dad turned away the neighbor boy. Apparently, he was only willing to risk our lives.

Lake Superior was a mirror as we set out. We could see our reflections on the surface and our long wake spreading behind us. Dressed in our ragged summer cut-offs, we looked like pirates, or at least the children of pirates. We shouted and sang, like five pi-rates will do, heading off for adventure. Even Mugsy, our little dachshund, went along.

I'm sure Mom and the neighbors could hear us howling and laughing far out across the calm water.

Pequaming was easy to spot from the lake. The old water tower could be seen on a clear day from the *Camp*, a distance of less than five miles. As we approached, we could read the *Ford* script painted on it.

Little Pequaming Bay was still and quiet, disturbed only by our voices and the chug of the motor. We glided gently in and nosed the pontoons up on the sandy beach.

Pequaming was a sleepy sawmill town when Henry Ford purchased it in 1923. Back when cars were started by hand, with a crank, they used a lot of wooden parts. By World War II, when steel became dominant, the town was shuttered. What we came upon, that day in 1965, was an intact ghost town. Most of the old houses and buildings still stood.

We walked through abandoned neighbor-hoods, past peeling picket fences. We star-tled a dozing owl, perched on the low branch of a maple tree. I'm sure it was surprised to see humans in town. We stood on creaky porches and peered through windows into cobwebbed, vacant rooms. It was like being in an old *Twilight Zone* episode. The doors were swung open at the church, as if in-viting us in to say our prayers, or confess our sins. We sat in dusty pews as Dad ap-proached the pump organ. His parents had made him take piano lessons as a child, and he could read sheet music. With the pipes mostly out of tune, we could still dis-cern the melody as he pumped out *Amazing Grace*. Mugsy howled at the sound of the organ. I'm not sure if it hurt his ears or he wanted to sing along. He had a few songs in his repertoire. At parties, he could howl along to *Happy Birthday*.

Finally, after several hours of exploring, we settled on the porch of the old general store and opened Mom's picnic basket. As we dan-gled our feet on the dusty street, eating our sandwiches, we failed to notice the sky turn-ing gray. But when the first drops of rain hit the dry porch boards, everyone took notice, even Mugsy. Weiner dogs hate the rain. We grabbed the picnic basket and ran for the

LIGHT HOUSE, EAGLE HARBOR

Eagle Harbor lighthouse in the Keewenaw

boat. We hurriedly shoved off, thinking that the boat's canopy would provide shelter. But the wind had picked up and the rain was now hitting us at a sharp angle. As we left the shelter of tiny Pequaming Bay, the wind cranked up like the thrust from an airplane propeller. The gray sky had now turned a dark, greenish black.

Perhaps Lake Baikal, in Russia, is a fine body of fresh water. I've never been there, but they're always comparing it to Lake Superior. Biggest. Deepest. Stormiest.

Stormiest?

How could any lake on this planet be stormier than Lake Superior? From the *John Jacob Astor*, wrecked at Copper Harbor in 1844, to the *Edmund Fitzgerald* and a thousand in between; they haven't built the ship that's impervious to its storms.

Not that we had to be told, but when Dad roared, "Sit down and shut up," we knew it was serious. I frantically tied Mugsy's leash to the railing but he ordered me back to my seat. Wind driven water was now coming out of the sky and off the lake at the same time. The picnic basket and Karl's Cub Scout cap were the first to go. Then the canopy. Then Mugsy. I dove after him. On my knees, reaching under the railing, my hand felt down the leash into the froth. Just then, I felt Dad's hand grab the back of my shirt. We each had our responsibilities. I pulled Mugsy back in, cradled him in my lap with one arm, and held to the railing with the other. That dunking had to be the worst moment of his life, and it was my fault for bringing him. I felt horrible.

Frankie, the youngest, was terrified. Held tightly between Jack and Karl, he sat with eyes clamped shut, not muttering a sound. We'd all heard mom's warning when we went out: "Protect your little brother."

Lake Superior rapidly gained energy. It tossed us up and down like it was trying to shake a bull rider off its back. It slammed us so hard I thought the boat would break apart. We were beyond soaked; we were being power washed.

Miraculously, the motor kept running. An early 1950s Evinrude, it sputtered a few times, but never quit. We'd all swallowed several gulps of lake water.

We were now somewhere in the middle of Keweenaw Bay, unable to see either shore. The boat made slow, uneven surges, pushing through the heaving swells. I could see Dad glancing at the bubble-compass and wondered how we'd be doing without it. If he kept us on a westerly course we were bound to hit land. If the pontoons were still airtight we wouldn't sink. But what if a rogue wave flipped us over? We were surrounded by rogue waves.

I'm not sure how long we were out there; I never once looked at my *Timex*. Eventually, as we neared shore, someone spotted a blinking light. It was Mom, standing on the beach, pelted by rain, clicking a flashlight. How Dad found the *Camp* in that churning, dark storm, we'll never know. It was one of those miracles that parents perform, that children can't comprehend. Or maybe it was just luck. He was an old Boy Scout, though. You could leave him deep in unfamiliar woods and he'd be sitting at the kitchen table when you got home.

As Dad rammed us on shore, we jumped off and scrambled for the beach. As a group of five brothers, we weren't into showing physical affection. But I have a clear picture of Jack, carrying Frankie safely to shore, etched into my memory.

Mom started to admonish Dad but he countered, "Do a head count; they're all home, even Mugsy." We ran for the safety of the *Camp* and its warm fireplace. As Mom got out dry pajamas, she asked, "Is everyone OK?"

Unable to speak, our teeth chattering from the chill, Dad answered for us, "They're fine, they've had their bath for the week."

I could break a leg and he'd tell me to "walk it off".

Mugsy and I had some re-bonding to do. In front of the fireplace, on a pile of warm blankets, I made promises: "No more crazy boat rides." If a dog knows you care about him, he won't hold a grudge.

That night, the boat took another beating. The tie rope was left loose and the waves smashed it against the rocks.

We didn't go boating for a week, having developed a new respect for Lake Superior. Part of the simplicity of childhood was washed overboard. We learned how quickly all could be lost. And that was the last trip we made across Keweenaw Bay. Maybe Mom did have some influence.

But soon, with Jack being able to pull the starter, we were back to cruising up and down the shoreline. Learning from Dad, he continued hitting logs and boulders and ramming it on the beach. By the end of summer, it looked like something gypsies had abandoned. Winterizing it consisted of winching it further onto the beach and removing the gas tank.

When school started, we regaled our classmates with stories of ghost towns. Of giant waves, that swallowed us up and spat us back out. How Mugsy was swept overboard, saved only by his leash. For once, we didn't have to exaggerate.

So, whatever became of our beloved pontoon boat, that took such a beating, but delivered us home safely? The next summer, when we returned to the *Camp*, it had vanished.

Gone.

Like my *Stingray* bicycle and so many lost fragments of my youth.

Did Lake Superior come up and grab it during the fall storms? Maybe. We like to think pirates stole it.

Dave Lehto was born and raised in the Copper Country, where he vacations every year. Though he is currently a licensed builder and artist in Traverse City, his passion is writing about adventures in the Upper Peninsula. For more of his stories, contact him at daveswriting7@gmail.com or 231-620-4857.

Your Invitation to join the UPPAA Today

MEMBER BENEFITS:

- Network with more than one hundred members of the publishing community
- Attend publishing/writing conferences and meetings
- Meet experts in the publishing industry!
- Receive the quarterly UPPAA newsletter, *The Written Word*
- Get discounts on IBPA and APSS Publisher Association Memberships
- Participate in the UPPAA email group for answers to all those publishing and marketing questions
- List your books & book covers at www.uppaa.org
- Display books at UPPAA tables at UPPAA meetings & other UP book events
- Learn the do's and don'ts of self-publishing
- Receive notice of upcoming book contests and awards
- Submit work for publication to the annual *UP Reader* magazine

Join now at http://uppaa.org/join-or-renew/

WHAT IS UPPAA?

UPPAA is the Upper Peninsula Publishers and Authors Association.

WHEN WAS UPPAA FOUNDED?

- The organization began in 1998 when Sue Robishaw, wishing to share her self-publishing experiences and learn from others, had the idea to form UPPAA. With the help of Lynn Emerick and Michael Marsden, the first UPPAA Conference was held in June 1998 at Northern Michigan University with thirty people in attendance.
- Since the organization's founding, UPPAA has grown to more than 100 members, representing a diverse body of writers in the fields of fiction, nonfiction, history, children's books, science and many other fields. You can view our members' books at **www.uppaa.org**.

WHAT IS UPPAA'S PURPOSE?

UPPAA was founded with the purpose to support and encourage networking and idea exchange among Upper Peninsula, and surrounding area, publishers and authors, and to promote books published and/or authored by UPPAA members.

DOES UPPAA HAVE MEETINGS?

- An annual conference is held in the spring and regular monthly meetings are also held. The meetings are held centrally in Marquette to provide convenience to members throughout the vast peninsula.
- The conference is usually divided into several workshops, focusing on such topics as writing, the mechanics of publishing, publishing cost-effectively, marketing, and publicity. UPPAA has also brought in internationally known guest speakers to its conferences, including Dan Poynter, Patrick Snow, Jerry Simmons, and Irene Watson.
- Attendance at conferences is free to UPPAA members.
- Members are invited to join UPPAA Board meetings on the first Thursday of every month in person at the Peter White Library (Dandelion Cottage room) or remotely via ZOOM.US livestream or telephone call.

HOW IS UPPAA ORGANIZED?

UPPAA is a non-profit organization with a Board of Directors. Board positions are open to any members and board members are nominated and voted in every two years by members.

WHAT IS UPPAA'S FUTURE?

With a group of enthusiastic and innovative members, UPPAA continues to grow and seek new ways in the rapidly changing world of book publishing to promote its Upper Michigan authors and their books.

Cut Me

by Sharon Kennedy

Tony wasn't sure what he should do with Maggie's body now that he had cut it into bite size pieces. He thought about frying it in hot Crisco oil, or maybe setting a match to some charcoal and grilling it. Hers was the third body he had sliced today, not literally, of course, just in his mind. Tony's mind was a mess and had been for years. His mental condition had something to do with being thrown into the trunk of a car and left there overnight when he was seven.

He was what some people might call a freak of nature. He looked like a boy but was old enough to be called a man. He had the hands of a woman. Not strong, manly ones that could drive an axe into a live oak tree, but delicate ones requiring only enough strength to squeeze the life out of his partners. Not literally, of course. Tony never took anyone's physical life. He was much too shrewd for that. He made sure his victims were mousey women who could tolerate being slowly squeezed.

Or suffocated. Tony loved to suffocate his partners. He did it slowly. So slowly they rarely realized what he was doing until they were deep into the affair and too afraid to find an escape, knowing full well he would come after them, find them, and coax them into returning. After a few years, his women became weak, mere ghosts of their former selves. They were unrecognizable when they looked in a mirror. Friends and associates didn't see the change, but the women did.

Death by cutting or suffocation was nothing compared to death by Tony's love. He loved some of his victims to death. Not literally, of course, but in his mind. He had a way of taking the hate eating his innards and reinventing it as love. He had a head for violence because that's what he was raised on. Not kindness or thoughtfulness or patience or nurturing, but violence. As a kid, he saw it every day. It was as much a part of him as his right arm. It was only natural he would equate violence towards women as a display of love. The first time he'd hit Maggie with her rolling pin, he assured her he loved her because if he didn't, he would have used the butt of his shotgun. The second time he hit her, it was with his fist. Maggie knew the pain in her jaw was proof positive of Tony's devotion.

The bizarre affair went on for years because Tony wouldn't leave and Maggie was too much in love to desert him. After all, he needed her. He told her every day she was his life and everything to him. "What would I do without you?" he would ask. Such words sent Maggie into romance heaven. Surely, he didn't mean to be violent. Maggie hated that word. Tony wasn't violent. He was just misunderstood. So, she stayed. Then one day, she came home from Christmas shopping and found Tony sitting on the couch with strings of colored lights wound around his wrists.

When she asked what he was doing, he took his eyes from Fox News and looked at her. His smile was one she had often seen.

It sent shivers down her arms and made her heart beat fast. Slowly he got up from the couch and without a word gently placed each hand on her shoulders. Then quietly he began to unwind the lights from his wrists and wind them around her neck. His movements were calm and deliberate. Maggie stood still as Tony talked in a soothing voice, telling her she was his Christmas tree. She didn't feel pain until he tightened the strings and the sharp little lights dug into her flesh.

She asked him to stop when the pain increased, but his monotone reply assured her he was only playing. He wasn't angry. There was no reason to be angry. She had spent her own money on gifts for his stepchildren. She hadn't asked him for money because she knew he had none. Of course, Tony had no money because he had no job. She had purchased an expensive knife set for his son, the only present the kid wanted. Maggie was happy to buy the gift and a dozen others for relatives of Tony's ex-wife. Maggie wasn't jealous. She was pleased she could be useful.

When a little trickle of blood escaped from her neck, Tony traced it with his finger. Immediately he unwound the lights and handed Maggie a wet rag to wipe her neck clean. As her heartbeat slowed, she realized how sorry Tony was and in a comforting voice told him it was okay. No serious harm was done. No scars would appear to remind her of the Christmas he tried to choke her because, of course, he hadn't. It was merely a game. He meant no harm.

The years passed and as in all long term love affairs, the ups and downs continued. There were good days and bad ones. Happy times when Maggie felt Tony's love with each physical blow he administered and sad times when he hurt her through his silence. The physical pain was soon forgotten and the bruises, scratches, and cuts healed without a trace of ever having been. Although Maggie would never admit it, the mental pain Tony inflicted was much worse because it was invisible.

Over his lifetime, he had perfected various techniques for emotional torture. The scars they left were unseen so they didn't exist, at least not to Tony. He skipped through the years, and everyone who didn't know him, loved him. He was a friend to all, quick to assist a neighbor with any task, and an all-around great guy. In fact, he was a perfect guy until memories of that car trunk crept into his mind. Then Tony became a monster.

He was afraid of the dark, of being alone, and of women. He huffed and puffed during the day, but if Maggie wasn't home when dark fell, he panicked. He turned on every light in the apartment. He turned on the television sets in each room, the radios, the stereo. When night came, so did the memories of his youth. Tony was a mistake, an oops in the dark during a moment of passion. Gert tried to abort him, but it didn't work. Even as a tiny group of cells, he held to her for protection.

Tony's first childhood recollection, prior to the trunk business, was watching Gert fry fish in a pan of hot oil. He was three or four when the accident happened. Of course it was an accident. Everyone said so. Tony simply got too close to the pan and it tipped. While he recovered from the burns, his mother sat at his hospital bedside. She wasn't like other mothers, Tony knew that, but he didn't know she was a free spirit and Tony's father was her third or fourth husband. He didn't know that either until he was older. He learned something else when he was a teenager. He learned, quite by accident, the man he called dad wasn't his or anyone's. He was just some bum Gert picked up when Tony's father packed his bags and left.

But Tony didn't know all this when he was recuperating. He only knew the woman sitting on the chair next to his hospital bed had hurt him. He knew it, but he couldn't tell anyone. So Tony kept quiet and learned a valuable lesson at a very early age. Keeping secrets to yourself is the best way to survive or avoid punishment. When he was well enough to return home, he never went near the kitchen when Gert was frying fish in a pan of boiling oil.

Maggie learned, quite by accident, that Tony liked to cut things. One afternoon, nine years into the affair, she came home and found him sitting on the couch watching a crime show

Hotel Northern in St. Ignace (1920)

and cutting her favorite dress into tiny pieces. The pieces were falling into a cardboard box brimming with other items of clothing from her closet and bureau drawers.

She recognized pieces of skirts and underwear, gloves and hats, nightgowns and knee socks, and various other articles that had gone missing over the years. Of course Maggie dared not express alarm or anger. She turned her back to Tony and pretended she hadn't seen what he was doing, thus giving him time to stuff the dress into the box and carry it to another room. When he returned, his body crushed hers against the kitchen sink. Just before Maggie passed out, Tony released her and returned to his couch.

Life passed as life always does, and everything remained the same except for the inward changes no one sees. Tony's favorite show was *City Confidential*. Sometimes Maggie watched it with him if it wasn't too violent. She still hated that word, but occasionally it crept into her vocabulary. Tony also

enjoyed watching the Playboy channel, not for the naked women, of course, but for the interesting interviews from which he learned having intercourse twice a day helped prevent testicular cancer. Once Tony learned this, there was no stopping him. Regardless of her fatigue or disgust, Maggie surrendered twice a day, every day.

When Tony took Maggie, it wasn't her he was thinking about nor was it the healing of any potential sickness in his body. The image in his mind was that of Gert and the man he called Dad. It was their naked, sweaty bodies he saw, for he had often watched them the summer he turned seven. Jake caught him peeking through the slightly open door and ignored him. Every morning Tony slipped quietly down the hall to his mother's bedroom. By the time he was eight, he had learned to service himself while watching Jake service Gert. Tony's entertainment continued until one morning his mother saw him peeking through the open door.

This time there was no pot of boiling oil to teach him a lesson and no car trunk to lock him in, but there was something much more sinister called isolation. From that morning on, Tony lived in an isolated world created by his mother. She ignored him. Yes, she fed and watered him much as one does cattle. Yes, she bought him clothes and shoes much as one buys a doggie sweater and boots for Rover when winter comes. She spoke to him when speech was necessary, and when he turned sixteen, she shipped him off to his biological father, a man who was a stranger to Tony, who didn't want him any more than Gert did.

Maggie knew some of his deepest secrets because Tony told her things he never had shared with other women. She stayed because she pitied him, loved him, wanted to heal him. Not change him, of course, for she knew that was impossible. Maggie just wanted to protect him from anything hurtful. She told him many times she would never leave him.

But as we all know, there's always a way to leave someone and it has nothing to do

Engraving of Waterfall on Lake Superior (1840)

with a physical move. In his own, misbegotten way, Tony loved Maggie. So each day he sat on his couch, watched Fox News or *City Confidential* or *Who the Bleep Did I Marry* and continued to cut her clothes into tiny pieces. It was the only way he knew how to show his love. As he neared the age of 75, his panic increased and his mind became more confused. Reality and fantasy blurred, crossed lines, and traded places. Tony realized he didn't know the difference between the two and that scared him more than anything.

One spring day, Maggie sat next to him and reached for the remote. She was tired of listening to the constant drone of news commentators. She wasn't interested in politics, only game shows. She thought Tony was asleep when she switched channels. When Pat Sajak asked Vanna to touch the letters, Tony jerked awake. In his confusion, he thought Maggie was asking him to touch the letters he had been dreaming about: LOSER. It only took him a minute to wrap his hands around her neck and press his thumbs into her throat. It only took her a minute to reach for the razor sharp scissors on the end table. While he choked, she stabbed. When he realized what he was doing and felt the sharp jab in his side, he released his hold, at which time Maggie withdrew the scissors. They never spoke of the incident.

Eventually, Tony stopped demanding intercourse and Maggie stopped talking. They watched television deep into the night. Occasionally, Maggie heated Crisco oil to the boiling point and fried fish. Tony always avoided the kitchen when the oil was hot. In their little apartment above a textile shop, the lights burned day and night and chased away loneliness, abandonment, and anything as bizarre as love.

And so they lived for the rest of their lives. a sad, weary couple each dependent upon the other, each too fearful to start anew. Each hoped the other would leave or die or just disappear into some nameless void and never be heard from again. But Maggie learned life isn't like that. She learned it tends to drag on and on like an elastic band with enough stretch and endurance to last forever.

The Demise of Christian Vicar

by Sharon Kennedy

Yellow Front store in Sault Ste Marie (1900)

Winter came and Vicar bundled himself into his coat, pulled his hat over his eyes, and walked toward the residence of Miss Ida White. Miss White lived in a rambling farmhouse situated on a deserted patch of land belonging to her deceased parents. Vicar did not visit Miss White, but merely looked through the downstairs windows into her library. He loved the soft, orange glow of the light from her fireplace, and he loved to watch as she sat in her chair and stroked her cat, read a book, or knitted a scarf. Occasionally, she glanced toward the window behind which Vicar was hiding. At such times, he held his breath, fearing he might be discovered, half hoping he would be discovered, but Miss White was not looking for Vicar or anyone. She was merely resting her eyes.

One bitterly cold night, Vicar stood his post much longer than usual. He did not mind the icy wind or the snow frosting his clothing and covering his sharp features. He stared as if in a trance at the lovely Miss White as she stoked the fire, adding a log now and then to feed the flames. She was dressed as if for a party. A red garment clung to her body, and a magnificent gold colored shawl fell from her shoulders. Fringe fluttered as she stood by the window, brushing aside the curtain and raising her hand as if to scrape a bit of frost from the clouded pane. Vicar held his breath, for he was sure discovery was, at long last, certain. He counted the minutes, but no discovery came. The object of his affection merely smiled into the darkness before allowing the curtain to fall back against the window. He went home, disappointed and yet somehow relieved.

Two eves before Christmas, Vicar dispensed with his duties as quickly as possible and headed for the farmhouse. The night air was fresh, cold, and invigorating. Snowflakes fell upon him like a thousand pieces of confetti. The starless night and hidden moon forebode an ugly end, but Vicar was mindless of everything except his mission. Tonight he would expose himself and express his devotion. Tonight he would ask Miss White for her hand in marriage. They had known each other for thirty-five years but had never spoken of their love. Vicar's heart was overflowing with affection.

He would wait no longer. He tramped through the snow as it deepened with each step.

But old habits die hard. Before knocking on her door, Vicar would—for the last time—peek through the library window. He would gaze upon the beautiful woman who would become his wife, his partner, perhaps even the mother of his children should she be blessed like Sara. The warm glow of her fire beckoned him, but he held back. His love was not seated in her chair, nor was she at her writing desk. Her cat was sleeping on the beautiful golden shawl carelessly tossed by the hearth, but where was Miss White?

Vicar ran from window to window. He passed by a bedroom, a dining room, a sitting room, and another room where he could see nothing for the lack of a lamp's glow. He began to panic and wanted to call out, but he knew the wind would silence his pleas. Perhaps she had taken ill or perhaps she was in the bath, although the hour was much too late for that sort of thing. He waited, mindless of the numbing cold enveloping his body, oblivious to the howling wind.

Vicar's thoughts turned to the summer day he first cast eyes on Miss Ida White. He remembered the warm sunlight falling on her hair, turning it from a drab brown to a brilliant auburn. He clung to the memory of her fragrance. To the very end, he loved the aroma of spring arbutus. He could no longer feel the cold biting his body. He felt only the tender touch of her delicate hand on his brow as she brushed a wanton curl from his forehead. He heard not the snap of branches as they collapsed from the weight of snow. He heard only her sweet voice as she sang from her pew on Sunday mornings. He must see her one last time, beautiful and pure, before he took her as his wife.

As Vicar peered through the window, he imagined her eyes looking back at him, penetrating his soul. It can't be, he thought. Has she found me out? He thought he heard her laugh, but it was not her laugh. No, the harsh, mocking sound could not have come from the throat of his beloved. The wind must be playing tricks on him. He gave himself over to the elements. The numbing cold penetrated his coat, found his bones, played tricks on his senses, and still he would not surrender. He saw flashes of a smile as he pressed against the window. It must be the snow. It had to be the snow. It could not be his lovely bride-to-be enticing him with her naked purity unsullied by any man. Snow suffocated him, yet he felt not the cold for the heat of his passion burned as white hot as any molten furnace. His sanity flew away. He pounded on Miss White's window, he yelled, but in vain. Only the frigid wind heard his voice, a mere whisper compared to the blizzard beating the life from him.

When Miss White awoke to a beautiful, calm morning, and found Vicar, she was not surprised. He was quite frozen, his long nose pressed longingly against the library window. She gave him a thorough look-over. "The poor fool," she said to her cat. "All he had to do was open the unlocked door." Before seeking help, she said her morning prayers and readied herself for the day. After all, Vicar was quite dead. There was no rush, no need to notify anyone of the corpse leaning against her window. No need to excite the good townspeople and create a scandal. As Miss White stirred sugar into her coffee, she wondered how she would amuse herself during the long, dull winter evenings now there was no Vicar to peek through her windows and stare at her loveliness. Perhaps, just perhaps, the next Vicar would be a little bolder, a little more adventurous, a little more human. Miss White hoped, as only a spinster can hope, that good fortune lay in her future.

Sharon M. Kennedy writes "Common Sense at 70," a general interest newspaper column that runs twice a week in the *Sault News*. She's been writing for the monthly magazine, the *Mackinac Journal*, for four years. Her "View from the Sideroad" is an eclectic collection of fiction and factual stories. She also writes a human interest piece for each issue. *Senior Wire Service* out of Denver distributes her "Common Sense" column to Baby Boomer publications throughout the U.S. Occasionally she writes outdoor articles for the monthly magazine *Woods-'n-Water News*. Sharon can be reached at 906-248-2602.

Warmth

by Bobby Mack

That evening, he started burning the books. The first ones to go into the fire were the slim volumes. Machiavelli's *The Prince,* was only 124 pages, which included the bibliography and an index of proper names. When the pages fanned apart in flaming waves, he tossed in Hemingway's *The Old Man and the Sea,* with its 127 pages. He was starting to get a good blaze, so *A River Runs Through It* was the next book to hit the fire. By the time Fitzgerald's *The Great Gatsby* was ablaze, the old man's hands were beginning to warm. Then he reached toward the stack of middle-sized novels, the ones with eighty-thousand words.

It had been almost a week since the old man had been snowed in; a prisoner in his own cabin. That year, the November snow had hit Michigan's Upper Peninsula hard. Hunters took very few deer that season, because most of them couldn't negotiate the deep and blinding snow.

The old man had shot a six pointer from his blind that was less than a half mile from his cabin. He had to hump knee-high snow to follow the blood trail. Several times he had to stop and catch his breath. More snow started to fall as he took his first break. By the time he took his next rest, the flakes had swelled to the size of poker chips. He would soon lose the blood trail. His only consolation was that he was heading toward the cabin.

He came to the top of a ridge. At the bottom of the slope, three wolves were tearing away at his buck. The sight sickened him.

He fired a shot, and the largest wolf squealed like a puppy before collapsing in the snow. The other two bolted away.

He leaned against a tree and took a cold and heavy breath. The excitement from seeing the wolves had winded him more than plodding through the snow. As he regained his breath, he realized he had killed a protected species. If it was discovered by the authorities, there would be a fine, maybe jail time.

The wolves had done a fast job on the buck. Most of the hindquarters had been torn away. There wasn't much to salvage. The falling snow had already layered the dead wolf's eyes with flakes that glittered in the refracted light.

The snow had drifted halfway up the cabin door. It had to be shoveled away before he could enter. The fire in the woodstove had gone out, and the interior of the cabin felt colder than outside. He started a new fire with old newspaper, twigs, and a couple of split birch logs. Once a healthy blaze had been kindled, he placed an oak log in the fire box. He sat in the rocking chair by the stove. Sleep overcame him as his body absorbed the warmth.

He awoke in the dark. Night comes early in November. The cabin was off the grid, no electricity. He lit a kerosene lamp and started another fire, using the last two logs he had left in the cabin. His nap did little to restore his energy. It would be a considerable effort to slog through the snow to the shed for an armful of firewood.

His brother, Hank, should've arrived by this time for deer season. The old man could use a hand now. He opened the cabin door and saw through the glass of the storm door that a new snow drift had formed, blocking his exit. It would be futile, he knew, but he tried to push open the storm door anyway. The temperature had dropped to below zero. He realized that it wasn't a drift of fluffy snow that blocked him; it was a huge slab of ice that had sealed him inside his cabin.

He sat down to think. Hank should've been here by now. If the snow was as heavy to the south, then maybe Hank had cancelled the trip.

He turned on his cellphone -*NO NETWORK*- flashed across the screen. That was no surprise. The reception was very spotty in his part of the woods, so most of the time he had to drive to town where he could always get a signal. He never would've bought a cellphone if the gas station in town hadn't removed the last payphone in the county.

The fire was getting low in the stove. He looked for something to burn. A small folding table stood in the shadows of the flickering lamp. The wooden legs were easy to break. He put them in the fire. The tabletop was too big to feed into the stove. It would have to be cut down to size. He needed a saw. All his tools were in the shed. If he could get to the shed where his tools were, he wouldn't need them because that was where he kept the firewood.

He checked his cellphone, and again, no network. In the bottom drawer of a cabinet he kept a hammer and screwdriver. He used the hammer to break apart an end table. The effort relieved some of his frustration.

"Stupid me," he said. At the rear of the cabin, he fired up the burners on the cooking stove. He lit the oven and left the door open to throw some heat into the chill. There was some relief with the next breath he took. Satisfied for the moment, he heated up a can of beans and ate them with some soda crackers while the stream of heat from the oven warmed him. Now he could relax and think. His contentment waned as he tried to remember when the propane tanks had been

filled. Was it August? He had what was left in the hundred pound tank, but how long would that last? Maybe, he thought, it would be best if he could strike a balance between the two sources of heat. He could shut off the oven to conserve the gas and stoke the woodstove with whatever furniture he could break apart.

With the screwdriver serving as a chisel, he split the tabletop into pieces small enough to fit through the door of the stove. He used the hammer to break up the four chairs from the dining table. The heat gave him comfort. He went to sleep. At four in the morning, he awoke in the cold. He lit the lamp and fired up the oven to provide heat while he built another fire.

Soon he had a blaze going, but he had used up all the wood from the chairs. He emptied the drawers of a desk made of pine and fiberboard. It was easy to break into pieces with the hammer, but it burned rapidly and didn't produce nearly the heat that the maple and oak furniture did.

More snow had fallen during the night. He thought of opening a window and climbing out into the snow drifts, but he soon shrugged that idea off. What good would that do? He'd be risking a heart attack, struggling against the snow and ice.

The sun came out and it brightened his mood. An hour later it was snowing again. He spent the day tearing off the trim and molding around the windows and doors. His hardest task was splitting apart the headboard from his bed.

By late afternoon it became difficult to stoke the woodstove. Too much ash had accumulated. He had to stop fueling the fire and let it burn out before he could remove the ash. As soon as the flames began to wane, he could see his breath. It was time to turn on the oven.

He stretched out on his mattress that he had placed in front of the woodstove. While the embers cooled, he took a short nap. He slept longer than he expected to. There wasn't any warmth from the oven. The tank of propane was spent. The remaining embers in the woodstove had dimmed. He shivered uncontrollably as he shoveled the ashes into

Calumet & Hecla Mine (1912)

a galvanized bucket. Now there was nothing left to burn but the books.

His ex-wife would've enjoyed the scene of watching him destroy what she called "clutter." He kept every book that he had ever bought, mostly from secondhand bookstores and garage sales. All the years of their marriage she would complain: "Why don't you just go to the library, get a book, and then return it?" His answer never satisfied her. "Sometimes I'll think of a passage from some book I've read, and if I want to refer to it, I want to have the book on hand."

He'd moved his bundles of books to his cabin after he retired. For the last five years he'd read and reread from his collected volumes, surrounded by the solitude of the forest.

The last book he placed into the flames was the *Random House College Dictionary,* 1598 pages.

•••

Hank had a local man plow the gravel road that led to the cabin. His brother's frozen body was curled up on a mattress. In his stiff grip were sheets of paper that looked like pages torn from a book.

Hank made the funeral arrangements. The undertaker told him what a difficult time he had removing the pages from the old man's hand. "He just didn't want to let go. They must've meant something to him," he said, "so I saved them for you."

With the help from a librarian, Hank learned what his brother had held. It was the first six pages of James Agee's *A Death in the Family.* Page 130 of Tobias Wolff's *The Old School,* and the last page of Norman MacLean's, A *River Runs Through It.*

Robert McEvilla is a retired stationary engineer who lives near Channing, Michigan. His fiction has appeared in the literary magazine, *Downstate Story.* Other short stories have been published by CWW Publications of Carmel, California, Twin Rivers Press of Ellerton, Flordia, and Toxic Evolution Press of Fairless Hills, Pennsylvania. His story, "Horseradish," received honorable mention in the *Glimmer Train* short fiction contest and was published. A memoir also appeared in *The Good Old Days* magazine. A novel, *The Goats of Santo Domingo,* was published by Wild Child Publications. The book is based on his experience with the 82nd Airborne during the Dominican Republic intervention.

U.P. Reader is Accepting Submissions for Issue #4

The *U.P. Reader* is an annual publication that represents the cross-section of writers that are the membership of the Upper Peninsula Publishers and Authors Association. This annual anthology will be used as a vehicle to showcase and promote the writers of the Upper Peninsula. Each issue is released in paperback, hardcover, and eBook editions in early Spring following the deadline. Copies of the *U.P. Reader* will be made available to booksellers, UPPAA members, libraries, and news services. The *U.P. Reader* has received more media coverage each year since the inclusion of the Dandelion Cottage Award. We hope the *U.P. Reader* will be a great place for you to showcase original short works, too.

Submission Guidelines

- Must be a **current member of the UPPAA** to submit.

- Submissions **must be original** with no prior appearance in web or print. Submissions will be accepted for **up to 5,000 words**. Writers who submit work which has previously appeared in blog posts, web pages, eBooks, or in print will be disqualified.

- Submissions **can be any type of genre**, Fiction, Nonfiction (memoirs, history, essays, feature articles, interviews, opinions) and Poetry. These also can include photography or artwork, but author must show permission for use.

- All submissions will be **reviewed through a jury** and the submissions will be chosen through this process.

- We prefer **Microsoft Word Document** (.DOC) files only or plain text files (.TXT). Do not submit PDF files. If you have some other type of text file, please inquire.

- **Authors may include photos,** with the understanding that they will be converted to black-and-white. We reserve the right to limit the number of photos per story. Photos should be at least 300 DPI and no smaller than 2 inches on a sided (i.e. 600px minimum). If the Author is not the photographer, we may ask for a simple one-page "Photo Release" form to be sent in.

The U.P. Reader will require FIRST time rights in print and digital. After one year rights will revert to the author. The UPPAA retains the right to use submitted works in perpetuity. For example, we look forward to the "Best of U.P. Reader" edition to be issued for the 10th anniversary.

Publication Schedule for U.P. Reader Issue #4

- Submission deadline: Nov. 15th, 2019

- Dec 21, 2019 Jury / peer-review process begins

- Jan 15th, 2020 announcement of selected submissions

- April 1, 2020, official publication date

Send submissions to submissions@upreader.org. Be sure to put "U.P. Reader Submission" in the subject line.

Welcome to Texas, Heikki Lunta!

by Becky Ross Michael

Another winter holiday passed with no snow in sight. Not one flake. That glorious white stuff hadn't fallen on Ella and Rae-Ann's part of Texas in years. The sisters searched the sky when cold winds blew. They peered out the windows to see what was new. Nothing.

"We had *such* fun playing in the snow that year," said Ella, pointing at a framed photo.

"I only remember making snow angels when I look at that picture," said her younger sister, Rae-Ann.

New Year's Day came and went. The children said 'good-bye' to winter break and returned to their classrooms.

•••

Mom shooed two dogs away as she sliced apples and spooned peanut butter onto plates for an after-school snack. Grandma sat in the kitchen, finishing her coffee.

"Y'all come to the table, girls. And don't let the dogs get your food," warned Mom. With a shiver, she turned the furnace up a notch before joining the others.

"It's sure getting cold out there," said Grandma. "I hear that Heikki Lunta might make a visit."

"Hay-Kee who?" asked Ella, licking peanut butter from her fingers.

Rae-Ann's eyes stole a quick look at the back door.

"His story's rather long," their grandmother said.

"Tell us," the sisters begged in one voice.

"Well, you know I used to live w-a-a-a-y at the tip-top of Upper Michigan," Grandma began.

"I sort of remember visiting you there," said Ella.

"That was summer. You have *no* idea what it's like in the winter."

Spindly Texas Snowman

Dogs Surprised by Snow

"Lots of snow?" asked Rae-Ann.

"Tons," nodded Grandma. "The snowbanks grow taller than people. Schools sometimes close for a week at a time because of the blizzards."

"Wow!" Ella exclaimed. The dogs cocked their heads to the side, listening.

"What does that have to do with this Heikki Lunta?" Mom asked.

"Quite a few families in Northern Michigan came from a far-away, snowy country called Finland," said Grandma. "Many years ago, those who lived in Finland shared stories called 'myths,' just like most ancient people around the world."

"I learned about myths in school," Ella said. "Those are made-up stories that explain how things work or got started. We read about how the elephant got its trunk."

"Exactly," said Mom. "And you've both seen a movie about Hercules, which is also a myth."

"That's right," Grandma said. "Many of those stories include gods and goddesses. 'Heikki Lunta' is like a snow god from Finland. People who live in Upper Michigan often talk about him in the winter when they're hoping for snow. Hotels and restaurants looking for visitors to the area even put up signs saying, *'Heikki Lunta, do your thing.'*"

"Did you ever see him?" whispered Rae-Ann.

"He's just pretend," Ella reminded her younger sister. "Grandma, why did you tease us and say he's coming here?"

Mom and Grandma exchanged knowing looks.

"The weather report says we might get a bit of snow tonight or tomorrow," Mom answered.

Her daughters' smiles reached from ear to ear.

"Make it snow, Heikki Lunta, make it snow," sang Grandma, when it was time for her to leave.

•••

When Dad returned from work, the sisters rushed out to his red pickup truck and told him about the forecast. After dinner, they drew pictures of their neighborhood covered in snow. At the bottom of hers, Ella wrote, "Please send snow Haykee Loonta."

The girls welcomed bedtime that night. Ella left her blinds open in hopes of seeing some flurries. In another room down the hall, Rae-Ann was excited and just a little nervous. She peeked through long lashes at her bedroom door before falling asleep.

While she slept, Rae-Ann imagined someone like Hercules. He wore a heavy white coat with its collar turned up against the cold. Ella dreamed of a man with long gray hair and beard, who was dressed in a flowing blue robe. Wind and snow swirled around him. Heikki Lunta? As the whole town slept, dark clouds gathered and delivered a bit of magic.

•••

At the sound of Dad's pick-up leaving in the morning, four eyes popped open wide. Rae-Ann and Ella ran to their windows and cheered at the sight of powdery snow on the ground and glistening flakes in the air. The time said 9:00. Why had their parents let them sleep so late?

"You're taking a snow day," Mom explained in the kitchen.

"School's closed?" asked Rae-Ann.

"The roads are quite safe, according to the radio. We don't get snow very often, so Dad and I decided to let you stay home and enjoy it."

"Yay!" both girls cheered, as they ran to get dressed.

"A warm breakfast comes first," Mom yelled up the stairs. "Then we'll hunt up our wooly hats and mittens. You'll need to wear your snow boots and not just those ropers."

•••

Light snow continued to fall throughout the morning. The three stomped trails in their backyard and built a small snowman. Ella and Rae-Ann lay down and flapped their arms to make snow angels. Their happy dogs rolled near them on the frosty ground. While watching their fun, Mom picked a torn section of blue fabric from a nearby bush.

"Maybe Heikki Lunta really *did* help us out," Ella said with a secret grin, at the sight of the blue material. "Does Grandma know about the snow?"

"I'm sure she does," said Mom. "Let's pick her up for a snow ride."

"What's that?" asked Rae-Ann. "A car drive on the snowy streets?"

"It's mostly melted from the roads. I'll phone her to say that we're coming, and then I'll show you my idea."

Ten minutes later, the laughing trio arrived at Grandma's apartment building. When she slid into the front seat, she saw what was causing their excitement. Sparkling snowflakes floated into the car from the open moon roof.

Mom pulled back onto the street. People up and down the sidewalks turned in surprise. Echoes of four voices drifted through the winter air, "THANK YOU, HEIKKI LUNTA!"

Becky Ross Michael often uses experiences as a former Michiganian and current resident of Texas for inspiration in her stories. When not busy writing, she leads a children's literature critique group and works as an online editor. Becky blogs at https://platformnumber4.com/ and encourages visitors.

Aiding and Abetting

by T. Sanders

Rex, who had more social disadvantage than Jack, came up with a suggestion they both could try to meet new girls...joining a fraternity. Skeptically, Jack agreed to give it a try. After two months of filling out applications that seemed to be half about sports experiences, no invitation to join was received. During that period, something happened that was probably a large factor in their poor reception.

In the earlier weeks of classes, Jack had noticed a girl in his physics class and he had seen her in the dormitory cafeteria. They had exchanged smiles and hellos in both places but never spoken as much as a sentence, until the dormitory beer party.

Jack had gone with little motivation other than thinking it might be entertaining to watch some of the inept residents drink themselves to the point of embarrassment. Ellen had gone to the party with a similar intent, but intending to cause embarrassment, not just to observe it.

With inhibitions lessened by beer, Jack approached Ellen and they mutually revealed elements of their histories and personalities. They found they both felt many of the same reactions, expectations and irritations about college life. Just as their proclamations of disgust reached a high point, two jerks from the dormitory interrupted them by first harassing Ellen and then intimidating Jack. That was all the inspiration they needed to devise a plan to retaliate against them.

The first step in the plan was for Ellen to flirt with the two "targets" simultaneously. When asked to dance, she responded as if both of them had just asked.

"I'll dance with whoever can chug one the fastest."

She had them stand back-to-back and declared herself judge. Result of the first round was close enough that no one objected to the call of "tie." The immediate call from the observing audience for a tie breaker was started by Jack. Rex unknowingly joined the conspiracy when he brought two more full and headless glasses. This time, without prompting, a now large crowd chanted "Tie... tie."

On a pre-arranged signal from Ellen, Jack shouted "Half-glass upside down." The predictable result for this round was that when each contestant stood up after swallowing twice as much air as beer, both were so dizzy that neither remembered the prize the challenge was for. As the two losers ran for the bathroom and outside, Ellen and Jack gave each other, a handshake, hug and surreptitiously blended back into the crowd.

•••

The next morning Jack stopped at his mailbox in the union and found a note saying "Thanks for last night. What we did was so satisfying. Let's talk about it after our next class together. See you then." Since he had not looked in his mailbox for three or four days and the strength of the innuendo was so overstated, he thought it was just another piece of crank mail.

Wednesday's Physics class found Jack tired and distracted after last Friday's party and a weekend of studying. Halfway through class he thought about Ellen. He turned to see if she was in class and was met with a straight on stare back from her with an enigmatic Mona Lisa smile. Walking out of the class, she caught up to him in the hall and asked "Did you get my note?"

"Yyyeaahh…" He stuttered for as long as it took for him to remember the note from his mailbox.

"Was there something wrong with it?" she said, sensing his hesitation

"No! Well yes. It wasn't signed and I'd never seen your handwriting before."

"Oh. Let's walk back to the dorms by way of the library. There's something I'd like your help doing."

During the time it took to walk to the library, the question of who was the naïve one of the two of them kept nagging at Jack. The wording in her note was the most articulate way of expressing gratitude for sex that he had ever seen or imagined. He was there and was sure that didn't happen so what was she about to ask?

At the same time the question was fermenting in his mind she was explaining the preface to her forthcoming request in a way that sounded like a prelude to an apology or a confession.

"Remember the other night I was railing at you about all the things I didn't like about college life? Well, an opportunity has come along that seems tempting enough for me to think about temporarily crossing a few of those personal boundaries I said I have. Would you give me an opinion on how big a hypocrite it would make me?"

"Sure…should I get some tissues to have in hand before you start?"

"No tears, I promise, or sex either…you can be as objective as a brother. I didn't tell you, but I've had a couple dates with a boy from the other male dorm. He's the athletic chairman of a fraternity and has offered to submit me as his fraternity's candidate for homecoming queen. I think I'd like to do it but wonder if it is selling myself out."

"Hey, go for it. You didn't make the social structure of this place. I still believe what you said the other night when you said that college social practices are mostly barbarian rituals. There are good people in fraternities and sororities, and a few years from now many probably won't list it as a high point in their life. For you it might be worth something down the road…if you become a weather girl or swimsuit model or something."

"Are you being sarcastic?"

"Actually, no…you are smart enough to avoid the bad possibilities, your boyfriend, maybe not. Doesn't he know that by supporting a 'dormy' for queen, he's risking ever again getting a date with a sorority sister? And, if you win, the only position he'll be eligible for in the fraternity is soprano in the glee club."

"You've almost convinced me to do it."

"Now you're being sarcastic."

"No, I'm patronizing you so I can ask the most important question. Will you campaign for me at the dorms?"

"Sure. That'll be easy. I'll bet every boy here thinks you're the best looking girl in the school. But with one condition."

"What is it?"

"That you let me guess who will be your escort when you win."

"Go ahead. Take your best shot."

"Dwight Wickersham."

"Right, do congratulations or sympathy go with that?"

"Only you will know. In any case, let the fun begin."

•••

On the way back from Ellen's dorm, two or three ideas for a campaign popped into Jack's head. He was apprehensive about any of them, because anything involving posters would necessitate getting permits from the student council. Rex was the dorm representative to the council, but Jack knew his involvement could be problematic. While trying to resolve the Rex dilemma, Jack came up with a fourth strategy that used one aspect of the competitive spirit that the "Greek" organizations prided themselves in having.

Jack calculated that the number of students in the dormitories was almost three times as many as there were sorority and fraternity members. If enough posters were put up in the dorms that identified Ellen as a dorm resident, the numbers advantage could do the trick. There were already six or eight sorority member candidates declared. If some fictitious candidates could be posted in fraternity frequented areas, the odds could be further improved. Since Rex could get the approved poster boards, the last thing needed was a dozen or so high quality pictures of collegiate-looking girls. Unexpectedly, Rex came up with the solution.

"Hey Jack, I know where to get pictures of college girls."

"Where?"

"The September issue of Playboy was the college issue."

"I don't have twenty to thirty bucks to get enough for all these posters. Do you?"

"We won't have to. You know the box factory about a mile west of here? Next to it is a sidetrack where they park cabooses. I'll bet there are at least a dozen Playboys in each one."

"Are you suggesting we break in to steal as many as we need?"

"No! We won't have to. My brother worked one summer for the railroad and he kept his pass key."

•••

Before they went to get the pictures, Jack ran his theory about how the fraternities would react to the attempt to subvert the election past the local sociology experts of the east dining room. These two, who were veterans and grad students, not only supported his thesis of how the fraternities would respond but exposed an animosity Jack was unaware of. It turned out that the collective impression the Viet Nam Vets had of the fraternities was they were a bunch of draft-dodging pansies. They even vowed to urge their buddies to take the time to vote for Ellen to further the cause.

Rex was right. In just two cabooses they got enough pictures of girls in college outfits,

or in at least parts of them, to produce fourteen posters. The hypothetical coeds were each given one of four names: Patty Will, Sally Wood, Megan Doos and M. I. Goode, along with Greek letter logos of non-existing sororities.

The last piece of the plan was an assumption that the school newspaper staff that was in charge of counting the votes and publishing the results, would not take time to verify that all the contestants were students, much less even real people.

Two days before the vote, they put up ten of the posters in strategic locations with four retained for replacing any that might be stolen or vandalized. Purposely, Ellen was not informed of the bogus posters, so her innocence of the effort could be claimed if she were accused. Rex and Jack continued canvassing the dorm public spaces, promoting Ellen's candidacy.

Before breakfast the next day, Rex and Jack went around to check on the condition of the posters, carrying along two each if replacements were needed. Amazingly, all were still there and only one was vandalized. It was easily repaired with a piece of white tape over the obscenity.

After classes and after the voting closed, they went back to remove the posters in accordance with the permit. To their surprise, none were still hanging. Their disposition would have to be determined later. All that was now left to do was wait for the outcome to be published in the school newspaper.

•••

Friday morning at breakfast, Ellen sat down at the table across from Jack and asked, "Have you seen the paper yet?"

"No"

She set down on the table in front of him a pre-release copy of the election results. He read from the article and from her signature smile that she had won... by one hundred twenty votes over the next highest candidate.

"I'm amazed," Jack blurted but then saw the expression on Ellen's face start to change, "that it wasn't by a bigger margin."

The real cause of his outburst was the name of the runner-up, M. I. Goode. For a split second Jack thought, "What would have happened if she'd come first?"

"I'm very grateful to you for the help," Ellen said with her happy composure returned.

"Have you heard any reaction from Master Wickersham yet?"

"No, but I'll see him this afternoon."

After she left, Jack started to worry that someone might try to throw out the election. Having carefully considered all points of view, he decided that the embarrassment of being played for suckers by a couple of "dormies" was enough for them to keep their mouths shut. As for his reputation, it was apparent there was no point in neither he nor Rex making any more applications for membership in a fraternity.

South Shore Railway Ore Dock loading freighter in Marquette

•••

The week after the school homecoming was mid-term test time. Jack did not have a chance to ask Ellen about the event until Thursday after their physics class.

"So how did last weekend go?"

"I would guess the ritual played out pretty much the way it usually did for say the last couple of decades."

"Did I detect the absence of the word 'fun' in your description?"

"Yeah, it started OK but really went downhill." The sigh that ended her one sentence summary signaled Jack she was catching her breath to give a detailed recounting.

Ellen went on to relate an evening of a few dances punctuated with sports statistics and reminiscences of the last two months' drunken bashes. To that point it was just boring, considering she had worked in her father's bar for her last two years of high school. But the last event of the night was a low point she didn't expect.

In accordance with the traditional script for the event, Dwight tried to grope her during the good night kiss. As Ellen aptly put it, "He wasn't going to get a shot at this piece of tail without getting a license first, or at least by asking before he went off half-cocked."

Jack almost laughed at the irony and sardonic humor in the way she put him down. Fortunately he didn't because it wasn't the end of the story.

Ellen's facial expressions changed again showing pain and disappointment as she continued.

"Yesterday I found out Dwight may have gotten what he really wanted for his ego after all. You know Rita, the queen of low-life, from my dorm? At lunch yesterday, she sat at the table with me. We've never been anything like friends, but she did what I'm sure she considered a favor by telling me something. She said her conscience bothered her enough that she had to tell me. Dwight approached her and asked her to do something for him. He convinced her to go in my room and steal a pair of my panties for him. I guess it was a trophy proving he got something from me that I didn't give him. The penitent smirk she gave me when I asked her how much he paid her to do it told me I didn't want to hear the answer. But I did and her answer made my skin crawl. Then Rita offered to pay me for what she had stolen."

Jack tried to express some sympathy for her situation but it didn't lessen the sense of guilt he felt for his part in it. Later, back in his room, the answer came to him just how to solve Ellen's problem. By the following day it was done but he wasn't able to let Ellen know until he found her in the lobby of her dorm that night where he happily told her, "I don't think you'll ever hear another disparaging word from Dwight."

"What makes you think that?"

"I'm pretty sure he was convinced to burn or destroy a certain item of clothing and stop telling any story that went with it."

"It's too hard for me to believe that rat would give up that easily. Prove it or I'll never believe another word you tell me."

"I had a friend who's in Dwight's dorm borrow the master room key on the pretense my friend had locked himself out. While Dwight was at class, I got in, found a pair of underwear hanging on the mirror and searched the room to make sure it was the only one. Then with a felt tipped pen, I wrote on the front of the pants 'THANKS SHORTY' and signed it 'Love, Rita.' For extra insurance, I spread them on the pillow of his bed so it could be clearly read and set his leather jacket next to them with the number showing. Finally, I took a couple of pictures with my camera, put everything back where it was and left."

Ellen looked at Jack with a blank stare for a few seconds and then broke into a laugh so infectious many of the others in the lobby joined in.

The last checkmate movement would be made by Ellen after Jack gave her the prints and negatives so that she could orchestrate their release however she wanted.

•••

Early in the next the semester, Jack got a call from Ellen. She had moved out of the dorms into an apartment away from campus. The call was a request to him to help buy and install a sliding chain door lock.

He had heard she was stringing Dwight along by accepting his invitations to fraternity functions that involved expensive dates without confronting him about the Rita episode.

Jack was at Ellen's door before noon with the lock, and twenty minutes later it was in-stalled. All the while he was mounting the lock, he noticed Ellen was staring out the window.

"Are you worried about this neighborhood?" he asked.

"No, it's someone from school I'm concerned about."

She admitted she had been "gold-digging" Dwight since the homecoming and hadn't yet broken it off with him. Just after starting the details of what had happened, she turned away from the window and said, "It's him; he's here."

Jack heard the door as Ellen buzzed him in and set the chain lock. Then she whispered to Jack to stand next to the door where he could not be seen from the hall. The dialog he was about to hear challenged the amount of respect he would have for Ellen from that day forward.

Sparing some distasteful details, it could be summarized as lame insensitive excuses to Dwight's question of why she had strung him along so far if she never intended to "put out." An unexpected gesture and a slammed door ended the scene.

Ellen, leaning against the doorframe, suddenly jumped backwards. Jack saw Dwight's forearm protruding through the still open door with an upturned hand in an open grasp pointed at a level six inches below her waistline. After those few moments, Jack felt two distinct emotions.

The first was, he realized Dwight deserved some amount of sympathy and now understood why he had developed very little physical attraction for Ellen.

Terry Sanders, currently lives in Manistique, MI, after retirement from work as a mechanical designer, environmental technician, and contractor preparing operation and assembly manuals. He received a BA from the University of Wisconsin. Publications include: *High School Textbook for Mythology*, short works of fiction, and a modern novella version of *The Iliad*. He has presented workshops at the 2nd Saturday writers group in Curtis, MI.

Three Roads

by Donna Searight Simons and Frank Searight

Three Roads - view from Brockway Mountain

In Copper Harbor two roads join,
Converging there to meet
This little piece of Michigan—
God's paradise retreat.
The first is Scenic Forty One.
It starts close by then wends
Its way to sunny Florida
Where pavement promptly ends.
We pass a well-groomed golf course near
The Mountain Lodge we like
Located past the Garden Brook
Where walkers come to hike.
Ahead we spy a pleasant lake;
Medora's calm today,
Yet crammed with sporting fish that bite
On bait that's tossed their way.
Soft breezes stir this tunnel road
Of richly verdant green,
With leafy canopy above
That shades the sylvan scene.

This woodsy, winding way provides
A roller coaster ride
Through valley glens and tree-clad hills
Where forest fauna hide.

Another drive that you'll enjoy
Is MI Twenty-six.
It's known for awesome vistas that
Are swell for scenic pics.
This Shore Road winds along the coast
Where frothy waves are seen
When mighty Lake Superior
Is turbulent and mean.
We pass small, craggy islands that
Above the surface reach,
And quiet miles along each stretch
Of sandy, golden beach.
It's best to drive at forty per,
Or forty-five, or more
While cruising down this highway near

The wind-swept, rock-hewn shore.
The Devil's Wash Tub is a spot
The tourists find quite nice—
A grotto carved in ancient rock
By water, wind and ice.
Both Hebard Park and Esrey are
Two places where a bunch
Of picnic tables wait for you
To sit and eat your lunch.
The towns of Eagle Harbor and
Then Eagle River slip
Into your sight, both adding to
The pleasure of your trip.
Stop at the Jam Pot, meet the monks,
They've breads that you may buy,
And then enjoy a scenic hike
To Jacobs Falls nearby.

A third way, Brockway Mountain Drive,
Is one route you will prize;
A branch road off of Twenty-six
It soars to scrape the skies.
Best not to race around the curves
Or drive too near the edge;

Most people stop and park their car
Some distance from the ledge.
Once there atop the mountain range
You'll see grand "postcard" views.
Snap lots of pictures; stay as long
As all of you may choose.
Now gone, the Sky Top Inn reposed
Where rocky cliffs are sheer,
A place where tourists stopped to buy
A crafted souvenir.
In Copper Harbor, meet with Sam,
A friendly guy you'll like,
Who'll rent to you a kayak or
Perhaps a mountain bike.

Each highway is so scenic and
A most delightful treasure
That having *three* of them is more
Than triple times the pleasure.
There is no other place on earth
Where *three* great roads provide
Us with majesty sightings and
A most delightful ride.

Three Roads - view from Brockway Mountain

Donna Searight Simons and Frank Searight are a daughter and father team who collaboratively wrote "Three Roads." Both are avid Copper Country fans and usually visit there each summer. Frank's mother, Dorothy, was born and raised in Houghton. Donna is the author of *Copper Empire*, while Frank has had numerous books published, including *Mystery at Copper Harbor*, *Dilemma at Lake Fanny Hooe*, and *Abomination at the Keweenaw*.

Young U.P. Authors Section

Once again, the U.P. Reader is proud to present the winners of the Dandelion Cottage Writing Contest. This is a competition open to all students in U.P. Schools, and is presented annually by the Upper Peninsula Publishers and Authors Association. Last year's winner was nominated for a "Best of the Small Press" award after it appeared in the *U.P. Reader*. Who knows what this year's winners will bring, but once again they are exceptional. So without further ado, here are our winners and stories:

- 1st Place went to Emma Locknane of Gwinn H.S.
- 2nd Place went to Lucy Woods of Copper Country Christian School
- 3d Place went to Kaitlin Ambuehl of Republic-Michigamme Schools

Emma Locknane is a senior at Gwinn High School. She enjoys hobbies such as writing, drawing, knitting, and daydreaming. Her favorite reading genres are science fiction, fantasy, and magical realism. She has many stories of her own she's working on, and often spends her time developing characters and fictional worlds. She also loves puns and cheesy jokes.

Lucy Woods is a junior at Copper Country Christian School, Chassell, Michigan. It is rare to find her not taking part in an adventure in the realms of her immense imagination, listening to music, or referencing movies. She also loves hanging out with friends, creating artwork with spray paint, and has a passion for acting.

Kaitlin Ambuehl is a senior at Republic-Michigamme High School. She loves reading and writing different works in the fantasy genre. She is an incredibly outgoing and social young lady who loves new experiences. Kaitlin has been writing for the majority of her life because she finds it to be a fantastic way to express her creativity and to relieve stress.

Trouble with Terrans

by Emma Locknane

Captain Bror didn't know what else she could do. A week ago, she'd thought that capturing the distressed human ship was a good idea; figuring it would be easy to make the terrans their lab rats, no problem.

She couldn't have been more wrong.

The matter began when the head scientist, Aldigo, requested an exploratory expedition to the solar system containing the human planet called "Earth." Though the Intergalactic Council of Research knew little about the terrans, Bror agreed to the mission anyway, despite the risks. Had she known it would become anything other than a simple investigation of the other eight planets, she would have stayed in the Shangri Nebula where the crew was originally posted, and she *definitely* never would have responded to that distress signal.

But there was no way she could have known this at the time, and so was now presented with a ship-wide conundrum of seven humans on the loose.

When Bror and her crew first captured them, they seemed docile enough. They were nervous, sure, but they honestly seemed more confused than anything, and even slightly grateful their broken and battered ship was no longer adrift in space. When Bror's crew trained their weapons on the humans, they were especially compliant; enough that they could be led into a cell reinforced with the highest-grade aluminum bars. There wasn't a doubt in Bror's mind this would be enough to contain the new lab rats.

Yet she was wrong.

The humans procured an escape plan in less time than an Earth rotation. The moment the guards took their eyes off the terrans, the group assessed their surroundings and escaped.

After locating security footage at a later date, Bror learned their plan wasn't complicated or an act of genius in the slightest. The humans merely wrapped their hands around the aluminum bars and pulled them apart. The captain watched in awestruck horror as the apparent alpha terran with short black and white hair and a nasty battle scar across one eye pried apart the bars of the cell with little effort. It was no secret some species could perform such an act of raw strength, but it left them drained and exhausted for a rotation. They wouldn't escape before guards arrived on scene. Yet this human showed no such weakness, and once free, beckoned the rest of the pack to follow as they wandered out of the cell block.

Bror's crew rounded up the humans for a second time. They were compliant when weapons were involved, and shuffled along to the maximum security cell Bror relocated them to. This one had steel bars considered unbreakable by various races in the galaxy, far stronger than aluminum. Bror believed it would be impossible for the terrans to escape this one. She was right this time. Even the eldest human lacked the strength to do so.

The problem was, they were smart enough to bypass the locking mechanism, and co-ordinated enough to make a run for it when the guards were on a shift change. Bror was clueless on how they'd managed to circum-vent the secret lock mechanism aboard the ship, though Aldigo hypothesized they like-ly watched the guards type the sequence code into the keypad on the wall. How the humans had the memory to remember the code long enough to escape while the guards rotated position remained a mystery to her. Nonetheless, the humans were corralled a third time, but it was obvious no cell would hold them for long. Even if they changed the security codes, the humans would be watch-ing for the sequence. To boot, the ship left Earth's system the moment they'd salvaged the human vessel. They ran the risk of more terran ships pursuing them if they didn't leave immediately. While they possessed su-perior technology to humans, enough terran forces amassed could be dangerous.

The trip had already exhausted fuel and resources, and was now too far from Earth to release the humans back into their natu-ral habitat. The humans' ship was irrepa-rable, so sending the terrans back out into space with a broken vessel and no resources seemed cruel. This, and Bror would rather bring the ship and its humans back to the Intergalactic Council for further study.

So, Bror gave the order: poison the humans and end them quickly. The captain was sad to lose such fine human specimens, but they just couldn't be contained with her ship's resources. If they were to be safely studied, it would have to be as cadavers. Thus, Bror

instructed Aldigo and his team to dart them, using the galaxy's fastest-acting poison, caf-feine. It was quick and painless, and would hopefully solve the crew's problem.

Except...that didn't work either. Once again, Bror was shocked by the humans' te-nacity.

Ten minutes, fifteen minutes, twenty, thir-ty, a whole *clock rotation* went by, and the hu-mans were *still* alive. In fact, they were even *more* active than before! For some reason, in-stead of convulsing and dying like other spe-cies, the humans became *excited*. The small ones let out strange, shrill squeals, running around and jumping on the adults mani-cally. Even the larger humans seemed more energetic. It was the exact opposite response that Bror and her crew had expected. Aldigo, for one, turned a sickly shade of purplish blue and looked like he was going to shrivel up and perish from shock. Even Sergeant Keein looked concerned, and Bror had never known him to be fazed by anything.

"So, deadly poison doesn't kill them?" Keein rumbled, cocking an ear as he looked downward at his captain. "What´re we going to do now?"

"I guess we'll have to try something else," Bror sighed, running a paw over her ears. "Maybe the Track Car?"

Aldigo gasped, black eyes widening with horror.

"*THAT?*" he turned a deeper shade of pur-ple. "Surely, you mustn't be considering such a thing?"

"What choice do we have? The poison didn't work. If anything, it backfired. We can't con-tain them like this. Soon enough, they´ll fig-ure out how to get out of this room, too." Bror sighed. "There's no other way."

"I'll prep the Track Car," Sergeant Keein grumbled, lumbering off down the hall. Bror exchanged a disheartened look with Aldigo.

"I'm sorry; I know you wanted to study them alive, but there's too much risk to the crew. If we can't contain them when needed, then it could be dangerous," the captain ex-plained. Aldigo blinked sadly.

"Well, at least we learned a *little* about ter-rans," he replied, his purple tint fading into a dark blue instead. "I'm sure the knowledge of their immunity to caffeine will be ground-breaking in and of itself."

"That's the spirit," Bror chirped, but then let out another sigh. "Let's get this over with."

•••

Thankfully, the humans remained relatively docile as they plodded through the halls of the spaceship. Granted, they were still moving as a pack unit despite the crew's best efforts to split them up into smaller numbers in case they chose to escape en route. This did not go over well with the humans, especially when Sergeant X'orph laid one feather on the smallest one. The tiny, brown-haired earthling let out a shrill yelp when he was pulled away from the others. This event instantly triggered an aggressive, protective response in the eldest female of the group, assumed to be the beta of the pack. Before X'orph had time to react, the adult female pounced the avian sergeant, tackling him to the ground and tearing handfuls of silver feathers from his body with ruthless snarls. The earthling she defended fled and cowered behind the alpha. Bror would have found the pack bond adorable were it not for the sinister glares of the other terrans. Said terrifying looks haunted her every dream for the next several orbits.

In short, splitting humans up against their will was a bad plan, and resulted in the severe injury of the sergeant. It turned out, humans had no rules against biting. Even now, the orange-maned beta was cradling the tiny earthling in her arms, making soft cooing noises to calm its whimpers. Bror and her crew found its cries rather grating, but they weren't about to become the next victim of the female's wrath, let alone that of the alpha. If that meant keeping them as a group, then so be it.

Bror and her crew reached the torture chamber. Even Sergeant Keein shuddered and wrinkled his snout at the sight of the Track Car; it was widely considered throughout the galaxy as one of the most feared torture weapons. Nobody wanted to get put into a Track Car; being dragged up and down, left and right, and even twirled *upside down* at ludicrous speeds while strapped into a metal car attached to a rattling track was thought to be one of the worst ways to go. If the panic didn't kill the victim, then the blood-curdling, brain-melting gravity forces would. This invention was so notorious that the sight of the Track Car alone would warrant an immediate confession from prisoners, not to mention hysteria.

But the humans, in typical fashion, yielded neither words nor panic. Instead, their faces lit up with amazement at the sight of the death machine, especially the smaller ones. They began jumping around and squealing once more, pointing at the contraption and baring their teeth in what Bror heard was called a "smile." This was confusing in and of itself; what kind of species used a threat signal as a sign of happiness? Even the adults looked kind of enlivened, though they appeared a little confused.

Bror and her crewmates were stunned. Keein and Aldigo gawked at the sight, mouths agape.

"Well, that's...not the usual reaction," Aldigo spoke, dark bulbous eyes squinting suspiciously. Sergeant Keein walked over to the humans, addressing the alpha.

"Oi, why aren't you afraid? This is a torture device, you know!" he barked.

The alpha terran looked at the sergeant like he'd grown an extra head.

"All due respect, Sergeant, but we haven't figured out how to communicate with the humans," Aldigo pointed out. "I doubt it understood what yo--"

Without prompting, one of the younger humans with curiously darker skin than the others repeated Sergeant Keein's exact words, going so far as to imitate his gestures and facial expression. Granted, it wasn't a perfect copy, for the human slurred a bit and messed up the finer linguistics, but for a species new to Bror's ship, it was a vocalized marvel; a huge leap in breaking communication barriers with the terrans. The discovery shocked the entire crew. The other humans seemed to think it amusing, and began chittering and chattering amongst themselves. Some of them mimicked the first human, and eventually all of them joined in, staring dead at Sergeant Keein as they continued to copy him. By this point, the crew understood this was mockery.

"...Load them into the Track Car," Sergeant Keein growled as he walked away, his eyes flaring an angry shade of red. Despite it all, Bror couldn't help but stifle an amused trill herself. Nonetheless, she contained her entertainment, and ordered the guards to prepare the Track Car.

Surprisingly, it didn't take a lot of time or effort to get the humans into the torture device. If anything, they jumped into it *willingly*. They even knew how to strap themselves in and smiled as they waited for the device to start, which made Bror wonder if humans were just naturally suicidal. Either way, there was, at least, the assurance the humans were okay with death.

Thus, Bror activated the device.

The car lurched forward, barreling along the track at breakneck speed. The humans roared and screamed at once, but it was not a sound of fear or terror, nor that of pain. As the car whizzed by, Bror could see the humans had their mouths open in wide, gleeful grins. All the way around the track, the humans continued their merry shrieking. For them, it was a sound of happiness and joy. But for Bror, it was the sound of *nightmares*; the call of creatures *so* insane that even death itself cowered from their snarly, toothy grin. As the Track Car came to a stop, the humans were still chattering in jubilation, and Bror knew that those shrill, raucous calls were going to haunt her sleep-cycle for the rest of her life.

"...It...didn't *work*?" Aldigo stammered, the bony red crest atop his head flashing a deep magenta in surprise.

"I can't believe it...! This...this is one of the most effective execution methods in the *galaxy!* How did it fail?" Bror shouted. "We even put it at top speed to ensure their death!"

The humans started hollering at Bror and her crew, pointing to the lever that activated the Track Car. Confused, Bror gestured to it as well. The humans began cheering and squawking in their gleeful manner, shaking their heads up and down. Bror felt sick when she realized what they wanted.

"They...want to do it *AGAIN*!?" she wailed, her black, pointed ears pinning back against her head as she bared her canines in shock.

"Huh. Maybe they know something we don't?" Aldigo guessed. "Perhaps they know it'll take more than one round to kill them?"

Could this species be any crazier? Bror wondered in bewilderment.

"So, send them around again," she ordered impatiently. "It´ll have to kill them off eventually, right?"

Thus, Sergeant Keein pulled the lever again. The Track Car shot forth, speeding around the track once more and eliciting the same shrill cries from the humans. Sure enough, when the car stopped, the humans just pointed to the lever again. This cycle continued on for quite some time before Bror came to the horrible realization that the humans weren't doing this because it would kill them, but because they thought it was *fun*; as if it were a *game*. The notion made Bror´s gizzard writhe.

"I can't believe this," Sergeant Keein huffed after nearly three clock rotations. "How are they still alive? *Nobody* can survive the Track Car!"

"Nobody can survive caffeine, either," Aldigo rebutted. "And yet here *they are*, alive and well after both."

"Ugh; there's just *no* way to kill them off, is there?" Keein slammed a fist on the railing, causing the humans to simultaneously turn their heads at the noise. Reluctantly, they were coaxed out of the Track Car, and were lined up against the wall. Rather, they were supposed to be, though Bror got the feeling the humans were growing less and less afraid of the crew's weapons, and may even believed this was some kind of joke. They ignored the armed guards and were busy chatting amongst themselves, consistently repeating the phrase "rull-er cooster." The captain resigned herself with a sigh. She didn't want it to come to this, but her options were wearing thin.

"In that case, there's only *one* option we have left to try," Bror spoke solemnly. Aldigo and Keein turned their gazes to her, curiosity gleaming in both of their expressions. "I didn't want to have to do this, but we'll need to use the Hydro-Chamber."

Everyone minus the humans gasped in horror; even the captain felt as if she'd used a curse word.

"What? Captain, you can't be serious!" Aldigo exclaimed, skin flickering a bright shade of yellow. "Hydro-torture is illegal in five systems for a reason!"

"I know, but what choice do we have? We can't contain them for longer than a day at most, I tried and failed to kill them quickly with poison, and even the Track Car didn't off them! And we can't return to Earth to release them now; we don't have enough fuel. There's *no* other way!" Bror explained. "I'm sorry, but this is how it has to be."

Aldigo faded to a dark shade of blue, but said nothing more. With a defeated sigh, Bror walked out of the room, motioning for the guards to follow.

•••

Shuddering as she looked upon the Hydro-Chamber, Bror couldn't help but feel a sense of guilt. She hated to be the person to sentence another species to such a terrible fate, but she couldn't think of any other solution to this problem. She had the guards lead the humans into the room, all of her crewmates staring ominously at the deep pit filled to the brim with that terrifying, clear hydrofluid.

It wasn't that the substance was instantaneously corrosive; many crew members consumed it in small amounts, but what made it so frightening was the slow death of submersion. Any longer than one clock rotation, and whatever unfortunate being that remained submerged would begin to dissolve. Hence, Hydro-Torture was singlehandedly *the* most feared practice in the galaxy. If the Track Car could instill terror with the sight of a machine, Hydro-Torture need only be mentioned by name, and prisoners *instantly* offered up their accounts, sometimes regardless of guilt. Nobody in the galaxy was willing to face the horror of melting in a pool of hydrofluid from whence there was no escape.

Unsurprisingly, the humans didn't seem worried. They kept looking between the hydrofluid and the guards like they didn't know what was happening. Their ignorance would have been adorable if the humans hadn't been so insanely durable thus far.

"Put them in," Bror barked, the guards grunting in response as they motioned to the pool. The humans offered one last confused glance at the crew before exchanging words briefly among themselves. Reaching some point of finality, the alpha turned and pattered near the Hydro-Chamber. He stared into the liquid a moment before dabbing a paw into the hydrofluid. He did this a few more times before regaining a flicker of previous excitement. He said something to the others, and the enthusiasm was infectious.

Encouraged by the alpha and beckoned by a wave of his hand, the others came forth to investigate. Bror watched, out of the corner of her eye, as one of the youngest terrans, male with a dark scruffy mane, leapt over the others and into the hydrofluid. The small dark-skinned human followed after, chasing the older one all the way to other end of the pool. The remaining humans roared with delight as they jumped into the fluid, hopping and splashing about. At the shallow end of the pool, Bror noticed the only human who hesitated was the smallest earthling, though he seemed content with the beta's presence. Bror made a mental note not to come between human females and their young; their maternal instinct held aggression more fearsome than any the captain had ever seen.

As the humans frolicked about the Hydro-Chamber, Bror noticed a few of the guards standing nearby, eyes wide with horror. Some were shaking, and others were changing colors at a rapid rate. Noting their fear, Bror sighed and waved them off.

"Go ahead. Sergeant Keein and I will remain. Everyone else is dismissed; you don't have to look upon this," she relented. Just like that, all the guards fled the Hydro-Chamber. Despite the dismissal, Aldigo remained. Bror found this odd, as unlike his militant superiors, he'd seldom come into contact with death, let alone that of such gruesome variety. For better or worse, Bror supposed, he was committed to gaining every last scrap of knowledge about the ter-

Tugboat Champion pulling 8 schooners from Lake Huron to Lake Erie

rans before they perished. It was a quality that, for better or worse, Bror had come to admire through working with the scientist.

And so, the waiting began.

As the minutes ticked by, Bror couldn't help but feel worse about the gruesome fate the humans were soon to meet. Half a clock rotation, and they were still frisking blissfully in the hydrofluid. They'd throw it at one another's faces, shove each other beneath the surface; it turned out they even knew how to swim. They weren't great at it, by any means, not by intergalactic standards, but they could swim. It was almost heartwarming to watch the beta teaching the little earthling how to paddle in the shallows, showing him the art. Even as time went on, the humans were no less aware of the danger and the fate yet to overcome them. Their ignorance was sad.

Except, when the clock rotation was up and the humans still showed no sign of dissolving, it appeared that Bror and her crew were the ignorant ones.

Another half-clock rotation past the limit, and the humans still showed no signs of absolute agony, no discomfort at all. In fact, the only notable thing that happened was the skin on their paws had wrinkled and shriveled a little bit, but it didn't seem to bother them that much.

Instead, the humans resumed their strange form of play. If they got tired, they'd perch on the steps near the locked exit gate for a while, but within minutes were back at it again. They never stopped talking the whole time, the young ones making awful high-pitched noises of apparent elation. Clock rotations went by, and while the terrans started to display less enthusiasm and give the crew prolonged stares, they showed no sign of dissolving into goo anytime soon. Their joyful chorus became a dull lull, and while some thought the humans might be weakening, Bror came to the realization their fading energy was undoubtedly a symptom of boredom.

And after a week of dealing with them, Bror knew what happened when humans got bored: they escaped.

"Let them out," she instructed, not sure why she was even surprised at this point. "It's not working."

"No way," Aldigo gasped, jaw hanging open as he stared at the humans, his skin turning a dark purple with shock and awe.

After opening the gate and herding the humans out of the Hydro-Chamber, Bror realized she was right back at square one. She had no idea what to do with the terrans; they were just so...*durable*. The way things were going, she doubted even her crew's weapons could harm them. If Hydro-Torture didn't kill these things, what *would*?

Certainly nothing Bror had on her ship.

"Well, now what?" Aldigo queried. "I take it we can't kill them, and imprisoning them seems a futile effort."

"Fine!" Sergeant Keein roared, irises burning bright red as he clenched his fists in a fit of rage. "If we can't kill them, we'll just have to teach them some discipline!"

Bror and Aldigo watched as Sergeant Keein, who was easily three times the height of the human alpha, marched over and stood in front of the humans, looming over their heads. At his throaty growl, they turned their heads up and met his fiery gaze. Bror couldn't help but take note of the slight apprehension on the humans' faces. She wasn't surprised; Keein's species was known throughout the galaxy for being able to win battles through intimidation alone. His people were some of the tallest and mightiest, and their sheer size often proved too much for any other species to surpass. Combine that with a harsh stare and a low, guttural grumble, and most never dared question his authority.

This concept failed to register with the humans, who weren't afraid of his size alone. The earthling, in all matter of karma, bared his tiny teeth in an exuberant smile and leapt from the beta's arms. The humans seemed to collectively stiffen as the small terran reached out and wrapped his limbs around the sergeant's fuzzy ankle.

"Wh-hey! No, no, no, no! Let go! Get off!" Sergeant Keein barked as he stumbled backwards, desperately trying to get the dwarfish, sopping wet human off his foot. The other humans clearly found this comical, and cackled as if they perceived this as funny. They only laughed harder when Sergeant Keein let out the most shrill, undignified yelp as he stuck his foot out in a desperate attempt to keep the little human as far away as possible. Since the sergeant couldn't attack or threaten the tiny one for fear it would incur the alpha's wrath, and Xenoporc knew what he was capable of, Keein had to settle for gently, yet feverishly, shaking the earthling to the floor. It backfired, and the earth-

ling proceeded to climb up his leg and onto his back.

Observing the fun, the small dark-skinned human decided to join in, latching onto Keein's other foot and holding tight, fastened to his ankle. Three more terrans rushed for a spot on the furry giant, grinning like madmen. Losing his balance, Keein was dragged to the floor and looked up to see them perched atop his frame. The lot of them pinned the screaming, flailing sergeant to the ground as if he was an amateur wrestler. The alpha and beta abstained from the action and stood by the wall. Their expressions showed their lack of viable concern, and they began to egg the others on. At first, Bror worried for Keein's safety, but upon witnessing the harmless play, realized he wasn't in any danger. The humans weren't fighting or inflicting pain. On the contrary, the terrans were giggling and chuckling as they did in the Track Car and Hydro-Chamber. She realized this was all fun and games. Granted, it was a twisted form of entertainment, mock-murder and rough play by nature. But Keein, as frantic as he was, was completely fine. Bror saw no reason to intervene, though she cringed at the thought of trying to stop such creatures. She decided to go along with it, and trilled in amusement as she turned towards Aldigo on her right.

"Well, do you still want to study them?" she asked. Aldigo blinked away his daze.

"R-really? I...I-I can-?" he stuttered.

"Sure; might as well. The more we know about them, the easier they'll be to contain if we have to, not to mention we might be able to find out a way to communicate with them," Bror stated. "But for the love of Xenoporc, just...*try* to keep them in the science wing."

"Y-y-yes, ma'am!" Aldigo chirruped with excitement, skin taking on splotches of bright pink. He loved learning about new humanoid species, he and his bunch were about to have a field day. "I will! I'll learn everything about them! You have my word!"

"Very good. Now, uh...how do we get them to stop assaulting Sergeant Keein?"

"Hmmm..."

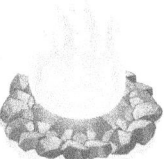

BEYOND BRAUTIGAN CREEK

splake

"sacred and obscene"

t. kilgore splake

new works from t. kilgore splake

"sacred and obscene"
&
beyond brautigan creek

TKSplake.wordpress.com

Stellae

by Lucy Woods

The seas be a treacherous yet beautiful maiden, whose secrets are far too many to be understood, but here be one I've come to experience meself. I have seen me a bunch a' misfits an' otherwise unrelated men an' turnin' them to the closest brotherhood they'd ever know. This be the tale of a crew such as this. It all started as I boarded the ship of Cap'n Williams, the greatest seaman known to sail. I looked about me an' me eyes fell upon a sturdy young man barkin' orders at a crew of about seven men hoistin' barrels, crates an' chests onto the deck. As I be walkin' closer to the sailor barkin' commands, there be no doubt that I caught his attention, for he turned toward me with his hand on his weapon an' called, "What be ye business here? Be ye one lookin' fer the Cap'n?"

"Aye, sir," I replied. The man looked me up an' down. I could only picture what he be thinkin' of me sun-worn coat an' me wearied boots. Finally, he spoke.

"What be ye business with the cap'n?"

"I got me a letter about a week ago from Cap'n Williams tellin' me to get meself here to Tamsworth an' find his ship, an' I'd be on me way on a dangerous voyage to get me for-tunes untold. So, I be lookin' for Cap'n Williams."

"Well then," he said, "I'll be takin' ye to the cap'n meself." He led the way into the cap'n's cabin. As we entered, I looked about an' saw a great many things. Straight ahead there be sizable windows that had thick curtains that be opened only to allow in the smallest bit of light aided by a rusty lantern which be settin' on a scruffed wooden desk covered with maps, papers, pouches of gold an' gems an' other such things one'd be apt to see on any sea cap'n's desk. I looked around an' saw chests, barrels, weapons, bottles an' trea-sures linin' the walls. Then I saw him, Cap'n Williams. The sturdy sailor approached him, an' they exchanged a few hushed words. The sailor looked more like a scrawny cabin boy standin' next to the tall, bearded cap'n.

"Ahoy, ye be James, aren't ye?" inquired the cap'n as the sailor went to his duties again.

"Aye, Cap'n," I replied.

"I be supposin' ye have a bit ye don't be knowin' quite yet, but ye'll come to learn in due time. For the moment we'll be hoistin' anchor an' settin' off rather shortly, an' I must have yer decision now. Ye can return ye back homeward, or ye can join as the newest member of me crew." I thought me a moment an' spoke with confidence.

"Aye, aye, Cap'n. I'll join ye crew."

"It be settled then. I'll tell Rigger we be on our way." We left his cabin an' the cap'n shouted: "Rigger, shove off!"

A shout came from above "Aye aye Cap'n!"

"Who be Rigger?" I asked.

"Rigger be me second in command. He be the fine sailor who ye've already had the pleasure a' meetin'. He showed ye to me cabin. After we be on our way, I'll have him show ye about Ol' *Abigail*."

"Who be *Abigail*?"

"Why, she be this fine ship. If ya keep her in shape an' cared for, she'll bring ye through anythin' an' will never fail ye."

•••

As I watched the land behind us slowly grow smaller, I heard me a voice behind me, callin' me name. "James!" I turned to see who it be an' saw Rigger swaggerin' over. "I'm to be showin' ye around." We walked about, an' he told me of the riggins', cabins an' me new crewmates. "Silvertooth be that sailor with the tooth about his neck. He keeps it as his trophy, it be from the first sailor he fought an' killed. He be the finest fighter to sail the seas, well, second to the cap'n of course. He at the wheel be Navigator. He be at the wheel most ev'ry moment unless he be readin' maps with the cap'n or eatin'. Over there be Chumchop. He cooks the grub. Silverfin, Jones, Pegleg, Four Fingers an' Brownbeard all run the riggings, sails, an' ropes an' have duties about the ship. Ye'll be workin' with them. Ye know me. I keep records an' be second in command only to the cap'n." Quickly the first days passed, and I became more knowin' of what me duties be. I keep the sails in good condition, help Chumchop catch food an' aid Rigger an' me other mates with the sails an' ropes.

•••

As we be eatin' our fish one evenin', I asked the crew where we be goin'. "Ye don't know?" asked Silverfin.

"We thought maybe ye was told in ye letter the cap'n sent to ye. He didn't tell us in ours," said Brownbeard.

"Even Navigator an' I don't know," added Rigger.

"Wait. The rest of ye got letters too? I be thinkin' ye be always his crew," said I.

"No, matey," asserted Navigator.

"We all got the same letter as ye," said Jones.

"The cap'n be assemblin' the greatest crew that ever sailed the seas to join him on what be a legendary voyage," said Pegleg.

"Back to the letters," said Four Fingers.

"We all got 'em about the same time as ye but we already be in Tamsworth, so we could be here right away. The cap'n be sayin' we couldn't set sail 'till ye came, an' ye did," said Chumchop.

"Why'd ye wait fer me?" asked I.

"Cap'n said we needed every sailor he sent for, that we all be havin' a certain reason or specialty an' that be why we motley crew be thrown together. Strangers from all across the seven seas brought together as the idea of a cap'n in the search of the greatest treasure known to man," answered Jones.

"But we don't know what this treasure be," Interrupted Four Fingers.

"I be thinkin' it be a palace of gold there for the takin' of whoever finds it," said Navigator.

"What be wrong with my idea of the greatest ship to sail the seas?" argued Rigger.

"I think meself that it be a cove of gems an' gold that shines like the sunlight when it be reflectin' off a calm sea," declared Jones.

"It might be the biggest carbuncle, the size of me head!" exclaimed Silvertooth.

"Or riches to last me whole life!" said Chumchop.

"Or the praise, respect, an' admiration of all sailors!" said Pegleg.

"Well, whatever it be, Cap'n Williams won't tell us," remarked Four Fingers.

"Why not?" asked I.

"Because ye all will be findin' out soon enough." We all jumped an' looked to where the voice be comin' from. It be Cap'n Williams standin' in the doorway with an eyebrow raised. He swaggered over to join the rest of us an' unrolled a large leather map in front of us on the table. It had upon it a great many things: islands, mountains, names, scribbled notes an' arrows. I had seen a great many maps an' been a great many places, but yet I could not see me a familiarity on this here map. "Here, men," said the cap'n, pointin' to a small island. "This is where we be headin'."

"Where be this island?" I asked.

"Right here, can't ye see where I be pointin'?" replied the cap'n with a twinkle in his eye.

"Aye, but I haven't seen any of those places sorroundin' it before."

"Of course ye haven't seen them. Very few have. It be a very dangerous place surrounded by treacherous waters an' risks unknown called the island of Stellae. Very few have dared to go. Only one has made it an' returned to tell of the beautiful wonders that be beyond these hazards an' here on this island, an' that be me." We all be starin' at the Cap'n in disbelief. We had heard stories when we be but children, an' that's what we'd be thinkin' they be, stories, much too good to be true.

Days passed an' turned into weeks an' weeks into months. We hadn't seen ourselves land since shovin' off at Tamsworth, but visions of what be on that island be keepin' up our spirits. Days be filled with sharin' stories an' trades with one another. One day, Silvertooth be learnin' me some fightin' moves as the rest of the crew be watchin'.

"Watch yer left!" said Rigger. I jumped to the right just as Silvertooth lunged with a knife in his hand, barely missin' me.

"How'd ye know he'd do that?" I shouted at Rigger.

"Easy, ye left it open as a perfect opportunity to strike ye. I be knowin' any sailor worth his salt would take advantage of ye there," he replied with a grin.

I ducked as Silvertooth made a swing fer me head, an' I landed me a good jab in his belly. Silvertooth doubled over, an' I, bein' concerned, asked if he be alright. He replied by quickly sluggin' me on me jaw. The ship seemed to spin about me as I fell to the deck. Me eyes stopped blurrin' only to see Silvertooth lookin' down at me with a grin.

"Nice work, matey," he said, offerin' me his hand. "Don't ever let yer guard down." By then I be standin'.

"I won't," I replied as I pinned his arm behind his back an' pushed him to his knees.

"Nor will I," he said. Quickly he rolled over an kicked me in the stomach an' jumped up. This whole time the rest of the crew be shoutin', cheerin' an' givin' advice.

"All right! All right!" said the cap'n, "A storm be a brewin' so we'd better batten down the hatches."

We all quickly ran to the riggin' an' prepared ourselves for a war against rain an' wind. By now I'd gotten me the hang of battlin' such storms. Before I'd never been so far into the open sea where such things be an almost every other day happpenin'. Me hands had gotten rough an' strong, me shoulders broad an' muscles hardened from fightin', haulin', hoistin' an' riggin' the ropes. Me changes weren't just muscular, but fer the first time in me life, I felt that I be belongin'. I had me brothers that be lookin' out fer me an' learnin' me all they know.

Thunder crashed with a flash of light. The wind started to pick up a great deal, an' rain started to pour an' drenched us to the bone. The boat rocked violently as we be doin' our very best to keep her upright. We fought the sails an' battened the hatches. We set anchors an' went to our quarters, dried off an' put on warm clothes an' met in the galley where Chumchop cooked up some grub. If it weren't fer fish an' Chumchop's skills an' creativity, we'd a starved weeks ago.

"That be, what, fifth storm this month?" asked Brownbeard.

"Sixth," said Silverfin.

"We'd better stop an' get some repairs done on *Abigail* soon," said Rigger, "She surely can't be up fer much more."

"Ah, don't ye worry. Ol' Abby hasn't let me down yet." said the cap'n.

"Cap'n?" I asked.

"Aye?" he replied.

"Will we be stoppin' soon? Chumchop ain't barely got nutin' to be eatin' but fish. I be unsure I can take much more," said I.

"Aye, ye be right. Besides, *Abigail* could use some help here an' there. Don't ye worry.

Marquette lower harbor (1861)

We'll be hittin' the port a' Cammonmouth in a week 'er two. In the meantime, ye'll have ta toughen up a little more, men." The next few days, we all kept an eye out fer land an' gulls as we went about our sailin'. The sea be gettin' calmer an' the air a little warmer.

A few more days passed, an' we saw the port straight ahead. It be small at first but then grew as we got close. A smell hit me an' hit me good. It be bread bakin'. I hadn't smelled bread bakin' since we left Tamsworth about three years ago. We docked *Abigail* an' stood on solid ground fer the first time in what felt like forever. We spent us about ten days gatherin' supplies an' makin' repairs on ol' Abby.

Months came an' went an' Rigger became sick. With Rigger out a work, we all be havin' to be doin' more about the ship. Brownbeard an' Silverfin be takin' care a the sails. Pegleg an' Four Fingers made sure nothin' be brokin' or needin' fixin'. When storms come or navigation be done, that be takin' care of by Navigator or the cap'n. Navigator ain't be very good at barkin' orders so seein' as I could hear about twice as good as any other sailor aboard, he'd have me be doin' his yellin' an' shoutin' fer him. It be a good way a doin' things but it still be not half as good as with Rigger. We all be feelin' like we had an arm taken off.

I'd spend me little bit a free time goin' an visitin' him. Somehow, even though he be feelin' the worst I think he'd ever been, he somehow still be the cheeriest of us all, still tellin' stories an' jokes like it be any other day. One day when I be bringin' him his supper, as I'd done fer the last week an' a half, I noticed somethin' that be different about him. He didn't seem to notice the sudden amount of light let in by the door.

"Ahoy!" I chimed. "Here I bring ye a hearty meal fit fer the cap'n himself, an' actually, made by the cap'n himself. Ye see, he be thinkin' he should try his hand at cookin'. Ha! He burnt half the fish we caught. The rest be made with very close help from Chumchop an' still we had to catch more just to get 'em close to resemblin' food!" I saw a wide smile spread across Rigger's face as I told him the tale, but it quickly ran from his face followed by a frown an' a sigh a' sadness.

"What be the matter?" I asked, handin' him his tray.

"I...I be tired of just lyin' here cooped up away from the crew. I want to feel again a gentle sea breeze on me face an' ropes in me hand. An' the stories ye be tellin' me, I want to be in them, to experience them meself, not just hear them," he said, thrustin' his knife in his fish.

"I see." I replied. "When I be but first becomin' a sailor, I broke me leg. All I could do was sit there an' watch the others climb up the ropes an' masts. It be torture when ye be small an' only wantin' to run. So, I can tell ye, I understand how ye be feelin'."

"Really? I be thinkin' ye said that ye ain't never broken yer leg before."

"Well, that's bein' because I never did break me leg."

He just looked at me with a smile an' twinkle in his eye an' said, "Ye scurvy dog, If ye weren't me friend, I'd throw ye to the sharks meself fer lyin' to me."

"Ha! I'd like to see ye try!" I replied with a grin. We laughed ourselves along as Rigger finished his meal. I started to take his tray but he held to it with a grip like iron.

"I think I'll take this tray to Chumchop meself." he said, startin' to stand. At first, he be a little dizzy, seein' as he'd not stood fer a while. I steadied him an' gave him me shoulder to lean on.

"Here we go," I said. We walked out onto the deck an' I could feel Rigger regain his strength as he smelled the fresh sea air. The rest of the crew who be goin' about their business, cheered an' greeted Rigger.

"Ahoy! What sailor be emergin' through yonder portal? Arr! 'Tis Rigger who we been waitin' an eternity to see!" yelled Jones, beaming.

"Rigger! Good to have ye back me boy!" said Cap'n Williams as he swaggered over to Rigger an' meself. "I order ye to never get yeself sick again." He spoke with a stern frown but a twinkle in his eye.

"Aye, aye, Cap'n, yer orders will be carried out!" replied Rigger.

Over the next few days he quickly got himself to full strength an' be as hard-workin' an' merry as ever which be givin' us high spirits, an' not a moment too soon, as we be gettin' to the dangers that be between us an' the island. The gentle breeze turned to a chilled gust. The cap'n said, "Here it be, men! Ready yerselves! To yer places!" The wind picked up, rain be startin' to fall, an' the sun hid itself. Fer hours we fought to keep her from capsizin' as the wind an' rain beat on our faces. Between the frigid cold an' the stingin' ice rain, every one of me bones ached somethin' terrible an' I struggled to see on account of the rain hittin' me eyes.

"Hang on!" I yelled. Other shouts filled the air but the rain muffed them too much to be heard. More hours came an' passed bringin' me to the end 'o me strength. Thankfully, the wind started to settle an' it stopped rainin', but it still be dark as night. The little light we got from lanterns be lightin' only the ship an' we could only see about a fathom ahead. I be lookin' about the ship to see what I could of our surroundin's. What the light showed was not much. I looked to the water an' it be clear as polished glass only to reveal rocks, broken remnants resemblin' ships an' weapons ruined by corrosion an' barnacles.

What I saw next made me shudder, then freeze in me boots. I saw a long scaly black an' green creature with teeth like swords an' eyes like fire. It be weavin' in an' out of a shipwreck makin' the ship look about the size of a toy that a small kid would play with. It stopped, tilted its head, then came straight at us. It be all I could do to scream, which caused the others to come runnin'. The serpent got bigger an' bigger as it be comin' toward us, its red eyes glowin' an' teeth shinin' in the light of our lanterns. The monster crashed through the surface an' its head flew over the deck. It's massive snake-like body seemed endless as it ran amidships. Suddenly, it be tightenin' itself an' the ship started to creak an' moan. Instantly, we sailors ran up to its scaly side an' tried to wack, cut, an' stab the creature, but it was all in vain. Then we noticed the cap'n who be dragin' over Chumchop's biggest cookin' pot.

"Don't just stand there, men! Give me a hand!" barked the Cap'n. Chumchop, Brownbeard an' Jones all went an' helped the cap'n carry the pot an' be placin' it under the belly of the monster. Rigger an' I understood what the cap'n be doin', an' we got some hay an' small pieces a kindling an' threw 'em in the pot. Silverfin smashed his lantern in there too, an' flames erupted from the mouth of the pot. The monster shook, an' it be loosin' it's grip on the ship. It quickly slid the rest of its body across an' off the ship an' swam away.

We all took ourselves a deep breath an' collapsed on whatever be the closest thing one could sit or lean upon. Fer some it be a close crate, fer others the wall or gunwale. Fer me it be the deck. I nearly fell asleep right there on account a me bein' so tired from the events of the last few days.

"C'mon men, *Abigail* must've gotten herself some damage o'er the last few days," said Rigger. "I know ye all be tired but so's ol' Abby, an' she's gotta' get us through so we need to put her first." What he said was already known an' be accepted by us, but we be so tired we needed ourselves a little reminder. Rigger got right to work, tellin' us what we are to be a doin'.

"Silvers," that be meanin' Silverfin an' Silvertooth, "ye check the deck an' see if ye can see any damage on her broadside. Jones, Brownbeard, Pegleg an' Four Fingers check the hull, holds, an' ballasts. Navigator, help the cap'n as he sees fit. Chumchop, do ye think ye can whip up somethin' to eat fer a much-spent crew?"

"Aye, aye, Rigger!" replied Chumchop.

"What will ye an' I be doin'?" I asked.

"James," he said, "ye an' I will be checkin' an' fixin' the riggin's, ropes an' sails."

•••

Some time came an' be gone as we all be carryin' out our assignments. We all had quite a bit to do, seein' as *Abigail* had a great deal a repairs needin' to be done. Some of the other sailors finished their checkin' an' repairin', so they came up an' gave Rigger an' me a hand. Thank goodness the weather settled down as the ol' girl couldn't take much more. When we all be finished, we feasted on a hearty meal that we all be needin' badly.

•••

It be still dark outside with a touch a fog as it has been fer over two weeks now. As we sailed on, we all be sittin' or standin' near our posts, ready fer anything yet still recoverin' an' restin' from the exhaustion of our long journey. "Up ahead! What do ye think it could be?" yelled Four Fingers as he pointed ahead an' above us at a point that seemed be some light shinin' through a cloud.

"Sink me!" gasped Brownbeard.

"It be God shinin' His kind face upon us!" said Jones. It be just the sun shinin' down through the dark clouds, but it be feelin' like God's glory an' grace shinin' on us. Gradually the light spread over the whole sky, an' what we saw in front of us be truly a beautiful sight. It be the island that we'd been waitin' to see the last four years. Huge mountains, surrounded by lush green trees, rose an' turned gray then white as they touched the sky. Birds be flyin' gracefully just over the trees an' a beautiful white sandy beach be outlinin' the edge of the water where it be meetin' the trees. We stood there, takin' it all in.

"Men," said the cap'n, "we've made it. Welcome to paradise. Welcome to Stellae!" Time flew as we quickly got to shore. It truly be paradise. Every tree there had somethin' fresh an' good to eat hangin' right there on the branches. We figured out that what we thought be sand before be tiny diamonds an' jewels with bits a gold mixed in. We all carried on like we be mere children livin' in a fantasy dream, swimmin' in clear lakes, eatin' like kings, adventurin' through the woods an' caves. I see now why the cap'n took us here: because without a crew that be as close as brothers, this place would seem to be mockin' yer lonlieness with all this richness an' pleasure but not a soul to share it with.

•••

After a while, we sailed on from Stellae an' went to many another islands, saw many a thing an' fought many a creature, but those be fer another time. All in all it be a wondrous journey that wouldn't have been nearly as good without me mates. The seas be a treacherous yet beautiful maiden, whose secrets are far too many to be understood, but here be one I experienced meself. I have seen me a bunch a misfits an' otherwise unrelated men an' turnin' them to the closest brotherhood they'd ever know. This be the tale of a crew such as this. It all started as I boarded the ship of Cap'n Williams, the greatest seaman known to sail.

Free

by Kaitlin Ambuehl

*B*roken, empty words.

"You're going to be alright." *I've heard that phrase so many times I've lost the effort to keep track.* Black outfits and the reeking combination of horrid cologne and perfume fill this once lively home. I stand next to their portraits, my siblings on the other side of me crying as more and more people give their condolences.

"We're sorry for your loss." *If only I could actually believe that. No one here knows; no one here sees.* My dead parents didn't have any family other than us, yet all of these relatives I don't know are claiming to be here in "our time of need."

"Is there anything we can do to help?" *You can leave. The only reason you people are here is because you want what my parents left behind, their money.*

More of the darkness, more of the cold.

The twins' sobbing continues as they look up at the portraits of our parents. Mom and Dad loved them with everything they had. Always affectionate, always worrying over their wellbeing. They tried to do the same for me.

I wonder when I wasn't able to feel their love anymore.

"What do you mean, there's nothing more we can do for her?" Memories that I tried to bury deep where they couldn't resurface have fought their way back up.

•••

"So what exactly are we supposed to do? Let her just... die?" Mom's tears, Dad's angry words, they yell at yet another psychiatrist.

"I'm sorry Mr. Blake, but your daughter... she's just..."

"Lifeless?" I finish the sentence for him, a dead smile plastered on my face.

"Octavia, please." I'm not supposed to be in here, but I was insistent on it. It's not the poor man's fault he can't do anything; he's not the first one to give up.

He won't be the last either.

"This is our daughter, sir. Please, there has to be something you can do."

"Well, we could always increase the dosage of her medications so--"

"No." I'm somewhat confused about Mother's reaction, it's hard.

"Maria--"

"I will not make her be a vegetable, Jonathan." Warm arms, a kind embrace envelopes around me.

"We'll always be here for you." *They lied.*

•••

"Go to sleep." I tuck the twins into our parents' bed tonight; both refused to sleep in their own beds after we got home from the funeral.

"Sissy... will you stay with us?" Pleading eyes, sad tears brimming in them, broken hearts burning their insides.

Eyes I can't understand.

"No." I close the door behind me, shutting out their whimpers that come through.

They deserve better. The hallway to my room grows darker and darker, the empty feeling weighing down my being.

I'm so useless. More pain, more hate, more suffering.

The bathroom feels like a freezer as I flick on the light and run the bath, the sounds of splashing water as it hits the bottom of the tub brings back a memory of the first time.

"Octavia? Are you home?" The voices that haunt me, the dreams that remain reminders.

"Are you in the bathroom? Come on, we're going to miss our reservation!" Dad's voice, warm and filled with laughter. The feeling of warmth from the tub, the smell of iron and blood.

"Octavia?" My vision is black, only faded voices.

"Octavia!" Cold hands collide with the warmth, the feeling of hot and cold burning my body, being lifted from the tub, hands remaining on my neck.

Just let me die.

The empty feeling inside eats away what little dignity, pride, selflessness, and hope you have left, and despite all the medication and treatments they give you, the emptiness never goes away.

"No one could understand..." I run my fingers across the water surface as I stop the rushing water, the stillness of it almost calming.

I slip out of my funeral clothes, soaking deep into the hot bath. The water holds a welcoming warmth, and I close my eyes to the bliss.

I wish I could understand. I wanted to be able to feel it, all of it. I wanted to be able to let go of the empty, the dark. But I can't. I never could, never will.

A glint out of the corner of my eye catches my attention. A fatal mistake on Mom's part.

Her razor blade. The dark forms around the corners of my vision as I twirl it between my fingers.

She forgot. She rushed to get out of here with Dad that day; she forgot to lock this with all of the other sharp objects.

The blade falls into the tub as I feel the plastic snap between my hands.

The glimmering blade shines against the light as I hold it between my fingers.

Can I ever escape this empty feeling? My fingers graze the rough, jagged scar across my neck.

Can I let go now? I feel the edge of the blade graze my neck, digging deeper and deeper into my fragile skin.

Is it okay? Just a few more seconds, a little more pressure.

I'll finally be free. Almost there...

"Octavia!" *That voice...* Hesitation, if only for a moment, listening carefully.

"Octavia, sweetie!" *Again.* The blade slips between my fingers, I fly from the bath and grab a towel. Dripping wet, heart pounding, I race down the stairs to the kitchen.

"There you are!" Shock, an emotion I forgot I was capable of feeling. Mom, standing in the kitchen, her face as beautiful as always.

"I want waffles, Momma!" *A* little voice, I turn. A little girl with long hair and big, gentle eyes bounces into the kitchen. Right through me, it's like I'm not even here.

What is this? I observe the scene, dripping more and more water into the puddle beneath my feet.

"Alright, but first, call your daddy inside." The little girl runs to the sliding glass doors, throwing them open. The bright light of the sun tears through my vision, the only clear image is Dad. He looks younger, less gray, no bags under his eyes from his countless nights awake.

"There you are, who's my favorite little girl?" Light, sweet laughter floods the room as he twirls her through the air.

Is this a dream? I watch as they sit and eat away at waffles, unable to see the water that comes off of my fragile frame.

Is this some sort of sick joke? A way to serve as a reminder of the things I lost?

Suddenly, it changes. Everything around me flies around, and now, the gray and tired expressions have returned to my parents' features.

"So what are you proposing we do? Let this continue on?" Anger, fear, and worry cloud Mom's expression; I remember this.

This was when I tried to kill myself. I remember their arguing, I remember the yelling and shattering of plates.

"Of course not, Maria! But you heard what the doctor said, there's no way we could've known."

"We should've helped her, Jonathan! We should've been there for her! Maybe... maybe if we had just tried harder to..." The tears I've seen her shed countless times before are different now. I think back to her smile.

No... That's not it...

"There's nothing more we could've done. Maria..." The sad, broken expression on Dad's face I know so well returns as he holds Mom.

It wasn't you... Pain, nothing but pain envelops my chest. It's agonizing, suffocating.

Please, someone make it stop...! I feel blood trickle down my body as my nails dig into my chest over my heart. The pain, my God, the pain.

"Look at you..." A pause, a moment of relief lets me breathe again. I look up, no longer in the kitchen. Instead, I'm in a hospital room. It's hot; sweat trickles down Mom's body, her face exhausted yet filled with joy. Then, a cry. A loud, obnoxious cry of a tender soul who's just entered this world.

"She's so beautiful..." Tears, but these tears are different. Mom and Dad look so happy, a face I forgot they could show.

"Octavia... Our baby girl..." Warmth, life, kindness. They tried so hard, worked so much. They gave me everything and more. They...

Quincy Mine's Man Car (1900)

They are gone... It's a typhoon, a hurricane, a massive storm that threatens to blow my entire frame away. Pain, agony, sorrow, *everything.* I can't breathe, I can't see. It's like I'm falling apart and coming back together all at once. Fleeing, flying, falling... I can't, I can't. It's all too much, too much to live.

"...Sissy...!" A voice, little and filled with fear. I break through, a tiny hand placed over my own. Tears, splashing across my already wet frame. The floor is cold and hard against my body, I'm back in the kitchen.

"Are you okay?" The twins, Damien and Carter, sit next to me, the towel covering my naked body from their sight.

"I..." My voice is shaking, my body coming apart.

"I..." Words aren't there, my throat sealed.

"I love you." Their warmth collides with my cold, their frames trembling as their cries and sobbing echoes through the kitchen with my own. I feel. *I can feel!* The emptiness, the disease that ate away at my being, it's gone. *It's finally gone.*

Mom... Dad... I miss you. I miss you more than words or actions will ever be able to describe, to tell. I love you, I loved you in every way I could. I just... didn't know how to show it, to feel it. But deep down, I never stopped. It was always there, always. I will never forget you. I will raise up the twins to be someone you can be so proud of.

Because now, now I'm free.

Young Writers Encouraged to Submit to 2018 Dandelion Cottage Short Story Contest.

Contest Rules

- Schools may nominate up to two short stories to represent their school.

- Home-schooled students may submit stories through their local school.

- Maximum length: 5,000 words.

- Authors must attend or be homeschooled in an Upper Peninsula School District.

- Teachers, parents, and others may offer suggestions and comments, but all writing must be the work of the author. In the real literary world, editors will offer suggestions. **This is to be a learning experience.**

- Teachers, parents, and others may point out spelling and grammatical errors on the finished manuscript, but the author is responsible for understanding and correcting all errors. **This is to be a learning experience.** In the real literary world, copyeditors will be correcting these errors. We expect polished submissions.

- Short stories must be submitted electronically in MS Word or PDF format

prior to December 31st of the current school calendar year to be considered in that contest year.

- Authors will retain the copyright to their work, but UPPAA reserves first publishing rights for eighteen months after submission. Selected works may also appear in a "Best of U.P. Reader" edition to mark our 10th anniversary.

Recognition

- First place winner will receive $250.

- Second place winner will receive $100.

- Third place winner will receive $50.

- Winning school will receive a trophy for display during the coming year.

Visit www.DandelionCottage.org for complete submission guidelines.

Becoming zen

by T. Kilgore Splake

quiet solitary spirit
oneness with
trees flowers insects
different colored rocks
constantly changing clouds

Good life

by T. Kilgore Splake

lawyers doctors businessmen
happiness buying things
houses cars furniture
expensive unnecessary luxuries
yet not enjoying life
always feeling empty
afraid to surrender
to living a simpler way
sleeping on futon
hotplate frying pan
single knife fork spoon
small coffee pot
sadly never becoming
person in their dreams

t. kilgore splake ("the cliffs dancer") lives in a tamarack location old mining house in the ghost copper mining village of calumet in michigan's upper peninsula. As an artist, splake has become a legend in the small press literary circles with his writing and photography. He is currently working on a new poetry collection titled "beyond brautigan creek."

Catching Flies

by Aric Sundquist

"Hey, Trevor!" Mark yelled. "Come check this out! Hurry!"

Trevor stopped in the middle of the overgrown trail and tried to pinpoint Mark's exact location. But he couldn't for the life of him figure out where his best friend had wandered off to. He took an educated guess and headed straight into the woods.

"Where are you?" Trevor shouted.

"Over here!" a voice answered.

Trevor swiped at pine branches and tripped over roots and eventually found Mark near a small embankment overlooking Ross Lake. It was a small lake, a mile in diameter, surrounded by spruce trees and marshland.

"What's up?" Trevor asked, breathing heavily.

Mark pointed down to his feet, to a plant with tiny leaves resembling folded paper plates. Long eye-lash follicles sprouted from the ends of the leaves.

"That's weird," Trevor said. "What is it?"

"I think it's a Venus flytrap," Mark said. "There's more near the shoreline. Go see for yourself."

Trevor moved quickly toward the lake, scrambled down the embankment and stood staring at hundreds of the same alien-looking plants. They engulfed the entire shoreline.

Mark climbed down and stood, staring as well. "Look at it all," he said, spreading his hands out wide and marveling at the plants. "It's like a whole colony."

Just then a tree frog catapulted off a lily-pad and landed on one of the plants. The leaves whispered shut, leaving a single frog leg wiggling outside the thick follicles.

"Did you see that?" Mark exclaimed. "I told you! It is a Venus flytrap!"

Trevor felt bad for the frog suffocating to death inside the carnivorous plant. He thought about helping it out, maybe propping open the leaves with a stick, but he didn't want to get too close to the thing.

But Mark had absolutely no fear whatsoever. He bent down close, his nose an inch away. "Get me a stick," he commanded.

Trevor rummaged around and eventually found a stick. He handed it to Mark, who stuck it inside and pried and twisted. But the plant wouldn't open. By this time the frog had stopped moving, either out of fear or it was dead.

"Damn," Mark said. His eyes darted around for something else to use. He must have seen something to his liking, because he moved closer to the shoreline. Unfortunately, his sandal caught on a partially submerged log and he tripped and tumbled down on his back.

A dozen trap-mouths clamped shut. Mark shrieked.

Trevor rushed over to his friend and helped him to his feet. "You okay?" he asked, wiping off dirt from Mark's back and shoulders.

"Yeah, I think so." Mark looked at his arms and legs, checking himself all over. There were a few scrapes on his leg, but no blood or welts or anything.

"Do you smell that?" Mark asked.

"What?"

"It smells...strange." Mark stuck his hands next to his nose. "It smells like honey and flowers and—" He sneezed.

"And what?"

"I don't know." He continued smelling his hands, then sneezed again. "It smells like raw meat and honey."

"Maybe that's how it traps its prey? By copying those smells?"

"Yeah, maybe." Mark laughed. "That scared the hell out of me!"

The sun was just beginning to set below the trees. It was time to head back home. They discussed the situation at length and decided to go back out tomorrow and inspect the plants some more.

They walked the rest of the way around the trail, making their way back to their bikes, fighting off a swarm of black flies. Mark kept looking over his shoulder, as if one of those plants was following him. Trevor looked, too, imagining a cartoon plant with this evil grin and swarming carnivorous arms tiptoeing through the woods while grabbing bees and flies and hummingbirds out of the air. And then it hid behind a bush every time he turned, laughing through dozens of green-razored mouths—all of which had just acquired a taste for human skin.

But that was all just his overactive imagination.

•••

The next afternoon, Trevor stopped over at Mark's house. A single pot stood on the kitchen windowsill with one of those alien-looking plants dumped into the dirt. Mark had obviously gone back and dug it up from the trail that morning.

"My dad said it is a Venus flytrap," Mark said. "We looked it up in the encyclopedia. But the article said they only live in North Carolina. Or maybe it was South Carolina. I can't remember. Anyway, he said I could have it as a pet, just as long as I took care of it."

"So, you have a pet that eats frogs?"

"Actually, it eats crickets and flies."

"Then why did it eat that frog at the lake?"

"See those little threads in the center?" Mark said, pointing. "There are six of them, three on each side. When something touches them, it causes the sides to shut. It doesn't matter what it is: a frog, a fly, a bumblebee. Anything touches it and they shut."

"Are you going to feed it now?"

"Yup. Just watch."

Mark grabbed a mason jar filled with crickets. He uncapped the jar and gripped one of the lethargic insects between his fingers, then dropped it on one of the leaves.

The cricket sat there for a second, stunned. Then it tried to move but the leaf clamped shut. It was like slow motion in a movie. Trevor noticed that when the plant closed, the leaves got thinner, so he wondered if they were filled with some sort of fluid, soaking its victim in something akin to white, hot lava.

Mark laughed. "See! It doesn't matter what it is!"

"It's kinda gross."

"What?"

"Watching things die."

Trevor thought back to earlier that summer. He had been sitting on his back porch, reading a *Spider-Man* comic when his neighbor's black cat trotted by. It held a squirrel in its mouth. The cat dropped the squirrel and the small animal tried getting away, but the cat pounced on it, tearing flesh and fur, squirrel legs kicking. The cat repeated this until the squirrel stopped moving, then jumped on the dead carcass and rolled over the mutilated body, pawing at it, picking it up in its teeth, throwing it back down. Trevor watched it do this for some time and realized how much he liked dogs. At least dogs ate their catch—a survival instinct.

"How did it get here if it only lives in North Carolina?" Trevor asked.

"I've been thinking about that."

"And?"

Mark grabbed a comic book—an old issue of *Man-Thing*. He opened it up and the cover had an order form for a living Venus flytrap. The picture looked a lot like the thing Trevor had imagined following him on their walk around the lake—a cartoon plant with razor teeth and an evil smile. It made him wonder if he had seen the ad somewhere before.

The caption read: Order your very own carnivorous plant today for only $1.00 each! Check or money orders only. Allow four to eight weeks for delivery.

"So," Trevor said, "somebody ordered some seeds from an old comic book and planted them out at Ross Lake?"

"Yup."

"Why?"

"I don't know. Maybe a joke or something. Do you want to see it eat a fly?"

Trevor was about to say "No," when Mark stuck his finger in one of the open mouths. The leaf snapped shut.

"What the hell are you doing?" Trevor said, grabbing his friend's arm.

"Watch and learn!" he said, shouldering Trevor away. Mark held his finger inside the plant for a count of ten, then pulled it out and held it up to his nose. His finger still looked normal—no cuts or slime on it. Then he sniffed it a few times and said, "Follow me."

Trevor followed Mark outside, out into the humid summer weather. Mark held up his finger and a swarm of flies engulfed his entire hand.

"They like the smell," Mark said. "It's a lure for them."

With enough flies buzzing around, Mark trotted back inside. Then, holding his finger over the plant, he waited for one to move to the tip of his finger. He tickled the thread-like fibers and the plant snapped shut, trapping the fly.

"Just like that!" Mark laughed. "Nice trick, huh?"

Trevor didn't say anything.

•••

School started the following week. The sixth grade. Although Trevor didn't love school, he was looking forward to seeing all of his other school buddies and hanging out at recess.

He had study hall with Mark for fourth period. Since it was the first day of school, they didn't have any homework, so the class was a little more animated than normal. It was also the day Mark and Trevor happened to catch a glimpse of Mary Olson's underwear when she bent over to grab a *National Geographic* magazine from the push-cart library.

"Hey Mary," Mark whispered.

"What," she said, turning to look him in the face. She was freckled and red-haired and became pretty when she smiled. She wasn't smiling now.

"Nice panties," he said.

Her face flushed the color of her hair. She turned away and pretended to be interested in her pencil.

"Hey Trevor," Mark said.

"What?"

"I got an idea." He motioned to Mary.

"What?"

"Catching flies."

Trevor was about to tell him to stop, but Mark had already raised his hand. He received permission to use the restroom and practically ran out the door.

The second hand revolved around twice before Mary turned to him. The coloring had left her face. She smiled and looked pretty again.

"Your name is Trevor, right?" she asked.

"Right."

"Can I ask you something?"

"Sure."

"Do you think he really saw my underwear?"

"I think when you picked up that magazine."

"Oh. Did you see?"

Trevor's smile gave him away.

She leaned closer. "That's okay. But...why do you hang out with him? He's mean."

"He's not that bad," Trevor said, feeling a need to protect his friend. "He just likes to pick on pretty girls, that's all."

Her eyes went wide. "What did you say?"

"Nothing. He just picks on girls sometimes."

"That's not what you said."

"I didn't—"

She laughed. "It's okay. I'll keep your little secret, as long you keep him off my back. Okay? Is that a deal?"

"Okay. I can do that."

"Thanks."

Just then Mark walked back inside the classroom, holding something in his cupped

Winter Train in Ishpeming (1909)

hand. Trevor could practically hear the flies buzzing from halfway across the room.

The term "catching flies," refers to one thing—going into the men's bathroom and grabbing a fly from the window screen. Once one is caught, you throw it hard against the window and knock it out cold, then tie it to a single strand of a girl's hair. When it wakes up, you have this fly circling around her head.

It was only a rumor, until last year, when Trevor had seen it done to a girl named Loraine Saari. She didn't know why the whole class was laughing at her. And then someone told her and she went running and screaming out of the room, the fly buzzing around her scalp. Everyone got in trouble and had to write, *I will not laugh and make fun of people*, one hundred times.

"Got 'em," Mark said, sitting down in his seat.

Mary turned slightly, knowing he was up to something.

"Don't do it," Trevor said.

"Why not? Do you like her? Do you want to marry her? Do you want to marry Mary?" He laughed at his own bad joke.

"Would you like someone doing that to you?"

"Let's see 'em try." He held up his fists like a boxer.

"Don't," Trevor repeated. "I mean it."

Mark sighed, but gave in. He opened up his hand.

Seven flies.

They weren't unconscious, and none of them tried getting away.

For the remainder of the hour Trevor kept an eye on Mary, hoping she would turn to him and give him a large grin. But she never did. Instead, she sat in her seat and waited patiently for recess, where she would be outside with her friends and maybe talk about the guy she had met in study hall who had stuck up for her when his mean friend tried to play a prank on her.

At least he hoped.

Trevor tapped his pencil on the desktop and kept watching the clock, ignoring Mark, even when he heard that first dry crunch between his friend's molars.

Aric Sundquist is a writer of speculative fiction. Born and raised in Michigan's Upper Peninsula, he graduated from Northern Michigan University with a Master's Degree in Creative Writing. His stories have appeared in numerous publications, including *Fearful Fathoms Vol. 1*, *The Best of Dark Moon Digest*, *Night Terrors III*, *Evil Jester Digest Vol. 1*, and the *U.P. Reader Issue #2*. Being a writer and a musician at heart, he also enjoys tabletop board games, playing guitar, and traveling with his girlfriend. Feel free to visit him at: http://aricsundquist.weebly. com/.

by Ninie G. Syarikin

You Are Beautiful

Whichever direction I face,
I see happiness.
A couple of doves flying side by side,
flapping their wings over the ripple of Portage Lake,
that is flowing calmly.
A boat dashing, cruising the length of the canal,
with the lone sailor heading straight with surety.
He's looking up, smiling toward the Sun,
that's kissing his lips in a spring afternoon, as if to say:
"This is a present to you, my son,
after bearing the harsh winter, ever."

Whichever direction I face,
I observe tranquility.
Assorted trees on the sprawling hills across,
are bursting their twigs,
thankful for the warmth that welcomes them.
Squirrels—grey, black and white—leap from branch to branch
with their S tails.
Wild rabbits hop from bushes to bushes,
playing hide and seek, chiding each other:
"Baby, don't go too deep, lest I can't find you."
"Mommy, come and get me,
lest Aunty Marmot discovers and takes me
to her burrow and feeds me with
sprouting mushrooms to grow me big, fast."
The Mother Nature smiles hearing this lovely exchange,
as if to whisper: "This is my gift to you, Little One,
for having endured the thickest snow all over."

Whichever direction I face,
I witness joy.
Children running around on the playground,
catching each other, filled with laughter.
Tralalalalalala . . . . trilililililili . . . .
With the spread of green grass, soft like moss,
soothing the tired sole of the ballerina's feet, like velvet,
with yellow lilies and daffodils emerging with pride,

swinging by the wind, as if singing merrily:
"This is my beauty for you to enjoy, Little Troops,
for having persevered through the long freeze."
Whichever direction I face,
I perceive optimism.
The chattering of the cheerful shoppers,
strolling in their summer sandals,
with their painted toe nails
along the Shelden Avenue of Houghton,
showing colorful displays of storefronts.
Red, purple, orange and pink reclining wooden chairs,
enticing the beachgoers soon bracing the season
on the shores of the Lake Superior.
Pretty mixtures of hues of intricate braided doormats
sold to residents, expecting their guests at home,
celebrating the rebirth.

Two friends stumbling on each other:
"Hi, Karen, long time no see, you look good."
"Oh, wow, Zainab, there you are my dear, survived!"
"Well, you have to; life goes on."
"Are you going away for holiday?"
"Yes, I am spending Ramadan with my family in Saudi."
"Good for you!"
The clear blue sky listening to this conversation with delight,
then generously stretching its canopy, wide,
as if sending a message:
"This is my reward for your forbearance, people,
for putting up with rain, hail, frost, ice and beyond,
not so long ago."

Whichever direction I face,
I feel Your Glorious Presence.
Humming
Hopelessly Majestic!
Impossible to escape
Futile to deny
Ungrateful to elude.
Piles and piles of black granite sands
Mountains rich with copper and rocks,
stones and pebbles plus gravels.
Stoic throughout millennia.
I am left gaping in awe:
"You Are Beautiful."

by Ninie G. Syarikin

The Snake Charmer

What do you remember from a misty summer day
in the town of Olenka?
A spread of delicious delicacies on a picnic mat
above the carpet of green grass
that I specifically prepared to welcome you?
When it suddenly rained,
we rushed to gather what we could
and took shelter under a big oak tree;
only moments later, running again to the prairie
to avoid the lightning that thundering.
A snake hanging with its fiery eyes,
protruding its branched tongue,
ready to attack.
Like an angel,
you caught its neck with your bare hands,
and admonishing the serpent:
"Return to the woods. Don't you ever bother
humans who are merely enjoying the nature here."
You released the sorry creature,
that slithered fast out of sight.
The picnickers were awed.

I heard that you go from village to village
to tame ophidian
I am also told that you never pass a place twice.
But, on this misty summer day,
I am hoping you will reconsider
I'll be standing here wearing yellow
in the middle of the sunlit meadow
If you see me, please stop by.

Ninie G. Syarikin works as writer, translator and researcher. She moved to the UP from Washington, DC in the fall of 2015 and has since been enjoying her life in the city of Houghton. She translates/interprets from English to Indonesian and Malay languages, vice versa, and writes in both English and Indonesian. Prior to managing her writing and translation business, US-SEA Strategy, Ninie worked for the US government-funded news organization Voice of America for 22 years and now federally retired. She holds an MFA in Creative Writing in cross-genre from The University of Tampa, Florida.

Summer of the Yellow Jackets

by Tyler R. Tichelaar

"For every thing that lives is holy."
— William Blake

May Dalrymple did not know quite when it began, but by early August, it could not be denied. There were more insects getting inside her house this summer than usual. In past years, there would be a fly or wasp or even a flying ant every week or so. May would catch them and put them outside. Over time, May had developed a catch-and-release program for insects and arachnids. Ants and spiders were easy to catch, winged insects a bit harder; the bees and wasps weren't too much trouble, but the flies, with their compound eyes that could see her coming, were nearly impossible.

May's technique was not complicated. She owned a large plastic see-through Coke cup she would place over the insect as it struggled against the window. Then she would slide a thin piece of paper or cardboard under the cup until the creature realized it needed to climb onto the paper or decided to climb up the cup's inside wall. May would then quickly flip up the cup with the paper over the opening, walk swiftly to the door, open the door, shove the cup outside, pull away the paper, and let the creature fly away, or for the crawlers, gently shake the cup so the creature would softly fall into the garden beside the back door. The process took little effort on May's part and was harmless to the insect, who could then return to the great outdoors where it longed to be.

But this summer, May's efforts had been forced to increase. Soon, it wasn't once or even twice a week that she had to play bug squad, but daily, and then multiple times per day. She had also noticed that the vast majority of what she was catching were bees.

"Where are they all coming from?" she would wonder aloud. It was becoming a real pain to have to stop whatever she was doing to rescue these insects, who too often were resistant to being helped. It would usually only take a minute or two to save them, but those minutes were starting to add up when she was busy all day running her antique shop, and then in the evening had to make dinner, or was going out with friends, or just wanted to relax and watch TV or read a book.

"Anyone else would kill you," she warned one frustrating bee that was very mobile and kept flying to another window as she tried to catch it. "You're lucky I'm so kind." It was true. Almost everyone she knew would have taken a fly swatter to these creatures, but May never understood how people could do so, even though, not six months before, she had been reminded that most people were not as tender-hearted as she.

While raising her daughter, Josie, May had not dated—both because she feared bringing a father figure into Josie's life, only to break both their hearts if he left, and because Josie had been such a handful, just a hair shy of being a juvenile delinquent.

After Josie graduated from high school and went off to the police academy—no one was more surprised by her decision than May—May had begun to date a middle-aged, divorced man named Ethan. She had liked him quite a bit. Ethan was tall and dark with just a touch of gray, rather broad in the shoulders, and since May was herself rather petite, being half-Vietnamese, she felt protected by his largeness. She had also thought he was sensitive—at least, he was good at listening to her. She'd poured out to him her whole story—how her American soldier father had gotten her mother pregnant while on a tour of duty in Vietnam; how he had been killed, and how her mother had proven May was half-American, gotten in touch with her father's parents, and arranged for her and May to come live in the United States; then her mother had died while May was just a toddler, leaving her to be raised by her grandparents.

May had shared with Ethan how difficult it had been, growing up in Marquette, Michigan, where at least 99 percent of the population were white, and how her grandmother had expected her to conform to American ways, with no opportunity to explore her Asian background. May had gladly conformed, opting to be the perfect granddaughter her grandmother wanted, complete with tea parties and an obsession with the royal family, and anything else that would make her seem like a WASP. But May had not been perfect—she had let herself be taken advantage of by the kind of white boy she thought her grandmother would want her to date—a young, upper middle class doctor's son from Grosse Pointe who was attending Northern Michigan University. When that boy learned she was pregnant, he dumped her and left May to raise Josie alone. Josie had been a handful, taking pride in looking different from others; even though she was only a quarter Asian, you'd have thought she was 100 percent Vietnamese the way she acted, and she never failed to mock her mother's dainty, All-American-Girl ways. Ethan had listened to all this long story, then told May she was beautiful, and made her feel relieved of all her burdens.

Not long after that conversation, May had invited Ethan over for dinner. She had been just about to put the roast beef on the table when a large spider scurried across the kitchen floor and startled her.

Hearing her scream, Ethan darted into the kitchen, grabbed an old newspaper, rolled it up, and flattened the spider.

May was in shock.

"Why did you do that?" she cried out.

"You were scared of it," said Ethan, grabbing a napkin to wipe up the spider guts.

"It just surprised me was all."

"Well, we don't want it getting into the food," he replied, disposing of the newspaper and napkin in the garbage.

"No, but it wouldn't have. I—"

And then she had burst into tears.

"May, what's wrong?" he asked.

"I just…I thought you were kind and sensitive…" she said, and then she grabbed the roast beef off the counter and carried it to the table.

She sat down, so he did too. She handed him the potatoes without saying a word.

He took them and said, "How was your day?"

"Fine," she said, taking a roll and buttering it.

He didn't know what else to say. After a couple of minutes of silence as he served roast beef and gravy to himself, he found the courage to say, "May, are you really going to be mad at me over a spider?"

"I…" she said, looking out the window, a tear forming in her eye. "I don't know how you can…can just kill something like that."

"You just told me the other night how I made you feel safe," Ethan replied. "I was just trying to protect you."

May picked up the bowl of mashed potatoes and dolloped some onto her plate without a word.

"May," said Ethan.

"Eat your food," she said. "It's going to get cold."

"May," he exclaimed, "spiders don't belong in the house!"

"No, but I could have caught it and put it outside."

"It's winter," he said, laughing. "Where would you put it? In the snowbank?"

"I could have put it in the garage."

"It would die from the cold out there, or more likely just find its way back into the house."

"So be it then," she said.

"May," Ethan persisted, "God made us custodians of the earth. He gave us the right to kill things when necessary. It's in the Bible."

May was speechless. Who was this man? She had only just met him last month. Obviously, she didn't know him well at all. She'd told him all about herself, but he really hadn't told her much about himself.

"May, you eat meat, don't you?" asked Ethan.

"Not very often," she said.

"Well, but you do," he persisted.

"I made the roast beef because you told me you like it, and even if I do eat meat, I'm not killing it myself, so it's different."

"It's not different," he said. "It's no different than when I go deer hunting and bring home a buck to make into venison."

"Deer hunting!" she exclaimed. "You never told me you hunted."

"Deer season was over by the time I met you, so it never came up."

May had not yet been in Ethan's house—they usually met at a restaurant. She had driven by his house, however, and wondered what it looked like inside. Now she could envision rifle cabinets and deer heads everywhere.

"May, it's the U.P.," Ethan continued. "Most men up here go hunting."

"No, I doubt most do."

"Well, a lot of them do. Probably half."

"I wouldn't know," she replied. She ate her mashed potatoes, but found she couldn't stomach the roast beef.

"Have you ever had venison?" Ethan asked. "I'd be happy to cook some for you some time."

"I don't think we should see each other anymore," she replied.

When May had told Josie about the breakup, her daughter had thought she was ridiculous. "You broke up with him because he killed a spider!" she exclaimed over the phone from her apartment downstate.

"I just didn't think he was the one for me," said May. "How can you be sensitive and still kill things?"

"I can be sensitive and still kill things," said Josie.

"You catch and free bugs too," said May.

"I did at home because you would have had a cow if I had killed them," said Josie, "but

I kill spiders now in my apartment, and I won't have any qualms killing someone if he shoots at me or commits a violent crime."

"That's different. That will be your job as a police officer."

"It's also my choice," said Josie, "to be in a job where I may have to kill someone."

"In any case," said May, sighing, "he wasn't the man for me."

May hadn't dated anyone since Ethan. Meanwhile, Josie had graduated and gotten a job in Marquette County with the state police. On a humid Sunday afternoon in August, Josie stopped by to see her mother. She met her at the door as May was about to release a bee.

"That's the third one this afternoon," May told her.

Josie rolled her eyes.

"Get yourself something to drink," said May, turning to go down into the basement. "I'll be right up. I just need to put my clothes in the dryer."

Josie went into the kitchen and pulled out a pitcher of lemonade. She was opening the cupboard for a glass when she heard her mother shriek, "Josie, come here quick!"

Josie rushed down into the basement, but her mother wasn't in the laundry room.

"In here!" shouted May. Josie went into the guest room. First, she saw her mother staring at the window. Then, she saw what her mother was staring at.

About fifty bees were walking up and down the inside of the window.

"What will we do?" May asked.

"Where are they coming from?" asked Josie.

"I don't know," said May. "I don't think they just accidentally got into the house. They must have a nest somewhere. What am I going to do?"

"Kill them," said Josie.

"We'll get stung if we try to catch them," said May.

"I said 'Kill them,'" Josie repeated.

"We'll get stung trying to do that too," May replied. "Do you think they built a nest in the basement?"

"I doubt it," said Josie, "but let's look."

They spent the next few minutes looking in the family room, the guest room, the little furnace room, and the laundry room. Josie found a flashlight and searched the darkest recesses of the rooms and behind the furniture, but no beehive appeared.

"They must have a nest under the siding outside," said Josie. "I don't know how else they'd get into the house." They both went outside and found a place where they could see the bees were obviously going in and out under the siding, but they did not see anything resembling a hive.

"What do I do?" May asked once they'd returned inside and were once again staring at the guest room's bee-filled window. "I can't have them in the basement like this."

"No, you're lucky you haven't been stung already," said Josie. "Wait, I have an idea."

"What?" asked May.

But Josie was already running upstairs.

May just stood watching the bees while waiting for her. "Bees, why'd you pick my house?" she asked them. "I don't want to harm you. Can't you go somewhere else?"

Then May heard Josie coming back downstairs accompanied by a clunking sound. In a moment, she reappeared in the guest room with a vacuum cleaner.

"What are you going to do with that?" asked May.

"Suck them up," said Josie, plugging in the cord.

"Oh, Josie," said May.

"Mom, I know you hate to kill them, but I don't want us to get stung, so the hose will give us distance."

Josie turned on the vacuum. May retreated into a corner; she would have cried over the bees' fate if she were not so terrified that her daughter might get stung. She watched first with horror, then fascination, as Josie held the hose forward, standing back as far as she could. She individually placed it behind one bee after another, sucking them into the vacuum. In just a few minutes, the window was bare of bees.

"Oh, Josie," said May, after the vacuum had been turned off, "I can't believe it. That worked."

"It did," said Josie.

But then May looked at the vacuum. It had a clear plastic container so you could see when it was full, but now it showed numerous bees crawling around in an inch or so of dust and lint.

"They're still alive!" said May. "Oh, let's take them outside so they can escape. They must be miserable in there."

"Are you crazy?" asked Josie. "If we open that, they'll all come flying out into our faces. Just let them die in there."

May looked like she was about to cry again, but Josie said, "Mom, be reasonable."

May pursed up her lips, trying to be strong.

"Let's go upstairs and have some lemonade," said Josie kindly. "We'll come check on them in a little while."

They had their lemonade and talked of other things. An hour later, Josie went back downstairs to check on the situation. May didn't have the heart to.

"A few are still crawling around in the container," said Josie, when she came upstairs, "and there were six or seven more crawling in the window that I sucked up into the container. You'll have to keep an eye on them and go down to vacuum them up every few hours I think," said Josie.

"I don't know if I can," said May.

"Mother, I can't be coming over here four times a day to vacuum them up for you!" Josie stated.

"I didn't expect you to," May replied.

"Then you need to go down and vacuum them up," Josie insisted. "If you're scared, put on some blue jeans and a jacket and gloves so you don't get stung. Then do like I did and stand back as far as you can—the vacuum's suction is good, so it will get them even if you're a foot or so away."

"All right," said May, realizing her daughter was probably right. "Oh, why did they have to pick my house?"

"I don't know, but you'll have to get rid of them or they'll be coming upstairs and stinging you while you sleep."

"I'll keep the basement door closed," said May.

"And tomorrow morning, first thing, call an exterminator," said Josie.

"I have to go to the shop in the morning," said May, looking for an excuse. She hated to kill the poor things.

Jack Pine Lodge near Shingleton (1940)

"Then call the exterminator from the shop," Josie replied.

"All right," said May, although she wasn't at all certain she would call an exterminator. Did her daughter think she was some modern-day Hitler that she would commit genocide on a whole colony of insects? And just how many bees were in a hive...could she kill thousands if it were thousands? But she also knew the other question was: Could she live with thousands of bees in her house?

•••

Before bedtime, May went downstairs. Sure enough, at least another fifty bees were on the window. "Forgive me, God," she said, and then she stepped over to the vacuum, turned on the hose, and pointed it at a bee. One bee after another was sucked into the vacuum. She watched with fascination as they tried to scurry up the window away from the suction—watched as their little wings fluttered before being sucked to their doom. She felt a horrible demon inside of her—a sense that this was fun, like playing a video game, like being Pac-Man eating ghosts and getting points for it. She was sickened that she could momentarily find it enjoyable, and when it

was over, she felt nauseous. She turned off the vacuum, then bent down in front of the plastic container and saw the poor bees crawling about in the dust.

"I'm so sorry," she said. "I would never want to hurt you, but I know you'll hurt me otherwise. Please forgive me."

Then she went upstairs and cried herself to sleep.

•••

In the morning, May woke with dread, the bees instantly intruding upon her thoughts. After breakfast, and before leaving for work, she went downstairs and sucked up another few dozen. Then she watched them crawl about in the vacuum. The bees from yesterday were all dead now. They had likely suffocated or died from being overwhelmed by the dirt and dust on their wings. The fresh bees crawled on top of their little corpses.

"I'm so sorry," said May, peering through the plastic at them. This time, as she watched them with fascination, she paid attention to the strange yellow stripes on their bodies.

"Are you really bees?" she wondered aloud. She had her cell phone with her so she googled "bee images," but the markings she observed

Lake Angeline Mine in Ishpeming

were different. She googled "wasp images," but wasps' markings were different also and their legs looked longer in the images.

"What are you then?" May asked her captives.

She googled "bees" again and found an article that referenced yellow jackets. She googled "yellow jacket images" and found her match.

"You're not bees at all," she said to her captives. "I'm sorry I'm so ignorant."

By this point, a few more had appeared in the window. She didn't know how they were getting into the room from under the siding, but she knew this problem wasn't going to stop any time soon. She was probably going to have to do what Josie had said.

May googled "insect exterminators Marquette, Michigan" and read about what they did—it was horrible—poisonous sprays—it was like putting these poor insects in a Nazi gas chamber.

"It's not your fault that you got into my house," she told her captives. "You can't help that you don't know any better. You can't help it any more than someone can help being Jewish...or half-Vietnamese." Her thoughts went back to bad memories of her childhood in Marquette, back to the late '70s and early '80s when her own grandfather had used the word "gook" to refer to her when talking to one of his racist friends—to memories of some older boys in her school who had made fun of her "pointy" eyes.

"How can I kill you?" she asked the yellow jackets.

Not ready to call an exterminator, May decided to head off to work, letting the three yellow jackets in the window remain. "They can enjoy a few more hours of life," she told herself. "If I only knew how to take off that screen, I'd open up the window and let them go free." But she realized if she did that, they'd likely only get back into the house.

"I'll figure it out after work," she told herself.

At work, she didn't say a word to her assistant, Barb. She knew Barb would just tell her to call an exterminator.

But in the afternoon when it was slow, May decided to read up about yellow jackets online. After a few minutes, Barb came up behind her and saw what she was doing.

"Why are you reading about yellow jackets?" she asked.

"They're in my house," said May. "I think they have a nest somewhere, maybe under the siding."

"You better call an exterminator," said Barb.

"I don't know," said May.

"What do you mean you don't know? You said they're inside your house."

"Just some of them," said May.

"How many is some?"

"A few dozen," lied May. "I sucked them up with the vacuum yesterday."

"A few dozen is a lot," said Barb. "You better call an exterminator."

"But I was reading online that they'll die with the first frost," said May.

"The first frost?" said Barb. "It's mid-August. We won't have a frost until October at the earliest."

"October 10th to 20th is usual," May said, quoting what she had just read.

"You can't live with yellow jackets in your house for two months," said Barb.

But May was wondering whether she could.

"Besides," said Barb, "they'll be back in the spring. Anyway, I need to know if you decided on how much we'll sell that old roll top desk for."

May and Barb went back to discussing business, but before May left the store that day, she had learned that while a yellow jacket colony will die in the fall, its newborn queen will fly away to winter elsewhere and start a new colony in a different location in the spring. That meant the yellow jackets would not be returning to May's house.

"It's only two months," May told herself.

•••

The next Sunday, Josie came over again. Her mother didn't answer the door despite Josie's knocking. May's car was in the yard, though, so Josie opened the door. Just as she did so, she had a horrible thought. "She insisted she wouldn't call an exterminator. I hope those bees didn't sting her to death."

Josie's fears were relieved when she stepped inside and heard the vacuum cleaner.

Going downstairs, she found her mother lowering the hose, having sucked up the last bee in the window.

May jumped, startled, when she turned around and saw Josie. Then she turned off the vacuum.

"Why won't you call an exterminator like I told you to?" asked Josie.

"I told you," said May. "They'll die with the first frost."

"And I told you that's two months away."

"I just can't kill all of them," said May. "There may be as many as fifteen thousand in their colony. I'll vacuum up the ones who get trapped inside the house so I don't get stung, but that's all."

"You're crazy," said Josie.

"I'm not crazy. I'm trying to be humane."

"Mother, even Jesus would kill them."

"I doubt that," said May. "And I'm sure Buddha wouldn't."

Josie didn't reply to that. She was the one obsessed with their Vietnamese heritage. Her WASPish mother had put her in her place.

After Josie left, May returned to the basement and told her captives, "The world is big enough for both of us. I'm sorry I had to capture you and that you'll die in the vacuum"—the vacuum was becoming quite full by now—"but you would have all died this fall anyway, and by only capturing some of you, I'm allowing your colony to survive longer so your next queen may be born and your line continue next year."

May sensed that the yellow jackets understood her. Their buzzing sounds actually had a calming effect upon her, as if they were communicating with her in some way—communing rather.

A few of the yellow jackets did make their way upstairs, but they were lone, solitary ones. May was glad for this because then she could practice her catch-and-release technique on them. Once or twice, one had landed on her plate while she was eating, but she had simply waved her hand to shoo it away; then it had flown to the window where she caught it and set it free. One morning, she woke up and could feel one crawling on her arm. "Get off me!" she cried, startled, and when she shook her arm, it flew off. She caught it and put it outside a few minutes later.

Never once during all these days did she get stung. "They understand," she told herself. "We are both doing our best to coexist."

•••

Finally, fall came. And with it, colder days. Each day, May went down into the basement once or twice to capture her house guests, and each time, she asked them to forgive her. She waited for the first frost, but she did not wish it to hurry, for that would be to wish ill on these creatures.

And then one mid-October morning, May woke to frost on the neighbor's roofs and dew on the grass where the frost had already melted.

When she went downstairs, a couple of dozen yellow jackets were still on the window.

Feeling a bit frustrated, she vacuumed them up without a word. Had everything she read about yellow jackets been wrong?

In the days that followed, she still had plenty of house guests, but in the next few weeks, the number gradually diminished. By November, she quit making multiple trips into the basement each day. Now it was only once every couple of days when she needed to do laundry or fetch something. When she did look in the guest room's window, she might see one or two crawling on the window that she would vacuum up, but just as likely there would be two or three corpses.

By Thanksgiving, she had almost forgotten about her house guests.

The first Sunday of December, she went into the guest bedroom and vacuumed up a couple of corpses. Then she finally emptied the vacuum into the trash. "Now I can finally vacuum the rest of the house," she said. She was grateful she had no pets that shed hair, for she had not vacuumed in a long time, not wanting to overfill the vacuum when she had yellow jackets to catch.

That afternoon, she was upstairs vacuuming a corner of the living room when she saw a yellow jacket on the carpet, struggling to walk.

"He must be the last one," she thought.

For some reason, she backed up the vacuum and let him be.

She forgot about that last yellow jacket until that evening. Then she went to see if he were still there. He was lying on his side. She picked up a piece of paper and was going to scoop him up on it to put him outside, but when the paper touched him, she saw his legs wiggle. She chose not to hurt or disturb him further on his deathbed.

In the morning, May checked on him again. The last yellow jacket had gone to his rest. May grabbed a Kleenex, and working it into a ball, gently picked him up and brought him to the garbage, where she gently laid him to rest. "Farewell," she said.

The Summer of the Yellow Jackets was over. It had been a long summer, extending into early winter.

It had been a journey. May did not doubt that if she had violently attacked her innocent house guests, they would have retaliated. She did not doubt that because she had asked their forgiveness, they had accepted their fate. She knew the newborn queen must be off wintering somewhere. May was grateful that she had helped to ensure the colony's survival.

A day or two later, Josie came over. As they were sitting and talking, and drinking hot chocolate instead of lemonade, Josie said, "Mother, something is different about you."

"What?" asked May.

"I'm not sure," said Josie. "You look—I don't know—you've always looked a little tired to me, like you were always exhausted from everything in life, but today you look like you're at peace with yourself."

"Hmm," said May.

But May knew Josie was right. The yellow jackets had changed something within her. She had once seen a play where a white character had despaired of ever becoming Japanese and committed suicide in the end. She had understood that despair, because she had always been trying to be someone she was not—to be a WASP and conform to the society around her. This time, she had done the opposite of what Western culture had told her to do. She had done what Buddha would have done. She did not know if that meant she'd get some reward in heaven, or whether it meant she would have to reincarnate fewer times. She only knew she felt good about herself and who she was and the universe around her. She had done the right thing.

And somewhere, May thought the Buddha was laughing.

Tyler R. Tichelaar is the author of nineteen books including *When Teddy Came to Town*, *The Gothic Wanderer*, *Haunted Marquette*, and *The Best Place*. He is also a professional editor and the owner of Superior Book Productions. Visit him at www.MarquetteFiction.com.

Help Sell
The U.P. Reader!

The popularity of the *U.P. Reader* is growing, but we need it to grow more.

Help us sell the *U.P. Reader* by selling the Reader alongside your other books. The *U.P. Reader* at its wholesale price allows those who wish to carry it to make a nice profit on the sales. Bookstores and individuals can all benefit from helping the U.P. Reader grow.

If you have writing that has been published in the *U.P. Reader*, you should be selling copies of the Reader alongside your other work. This not only helps get exposure for your writing but for all the others that were accepted alongside yours. Part of the mission of the *U.P. Reader* is to get the many voices of the writers of the UPPAA in a single publication so that readers would have a place to find and sample the incredible talent that makes up the authors and poets of the Upper Peninsula.

Taking a few Readers to an event can make the difference in selling. Those who have been selling the U.P. Reader have seen good sales and considerable interest in the publication from readers and customers. Many customers ask the seller if they have a piece in the book to sign it. As the U.P. Reader is helping you as a writer, you can be helping the *U.P. Reader*.

Do you have local booksellers in your area? Encourage them to stock the *U.P. Reader*. Bookstores that are selling the Reader are seeing brisk sales. Many of the bookstores have restocked their issues several times and are saying how much they enjoy them. They are profitable and returnable. The *U.P. Reader* is a win-win situation for bookstores.

Take a copy of the U.P. Reader to your child's English or Language Arts teacher. The Dandelion Cottage Award is open to all children in U.P. schools and homeschool. There is never a fee to participate!

Back issues of the *U.P. Reader* are also still available. They can still be ordered right alongside the new issue and can be combined to sell as a set. There are many who still haven't discovered the U.P. Reader yet, and a package set is a nice way to introduce them to the joys reading a Reader. These can still be purchased wholesale just like the current issue.

There are hardcover versions of the *U.P. Reader* as well. These are beautiful bound versions of the *U.P. Reader* that are a wonderful keepsake for the real *U.P. Reader* fan. Again, these can be ordered wholesale and sold right alongside the paperback versions.

To order, go to UPReader.org/publications on the web and put in your order. Contributing authors will be emailed a discount code and their orders will be discounted to the wholesale price (50% Off!).

Please help us, help you make the *U.P. Reader* a success!

Come join
UPPAA Online!

The UPPAA maintains an online presence on several social media areas. To get the most out of your UPPAA membership, be sure to visit, "like," and share these destinations and posts whenever possible!

Web Sites
- **www.UPPAA.org**: learn about meetings, publicity opportunities, publicize your own author events, add your book to the catalog page, read newsletter archive.
- **www.UPReader.org**: complete details about deadlines, submission guidelines, how to place a print advertisement, where to buy U.P. Reader locally, and more.

Facebook Pages
- **UPPAA**: www.facebook.com/UPSISU/ —OR—type in **@UPSISU** into the Facebook "search" bar
- **UP Reader**: www.facebook.com/upreaders/ —OR— type in **@UPreader** into the Facebook "search" bar

Twitter
- Message to **@UP_Authors** or visit https://twitter.com/UP_Authors

U.P. Reader — Issue #1

Featuring

"The Song of Minnehaha" by Larry Buege

"Fragile Blossoms" by Deborah K. Frontiera

"Winning Ticket" by James M. Jackson

"Stocking Up" by Janeen Pergrin Rastall

"We Are Three Widows" by Sharon M. Kennedy

"UP Road Trips" by Jan Kellis

"The Story-Seer by Amy Klco

"Lonely Road" by Becky Ross Michael

"An Abandoned Dream" by Elizabeth Fust

"J'acqui, Marilyn, & Shelly" by Terry Sanders

"Marquette Medium by Tyler Tichelaar

"The House on Blakely Hill by Mikel B. Classen

"Hoffentot Magic by Roslyn Elena McGrath

"Wolf Woman by Ann Dallman

"Menominee County/My Hometown Abandoned by Ann Dallman"

"Nonetheless" and "At Camp" by Christine Saari

"Katydids by Aimée Bissonett

"Source by Frank Farwel

"A Tribute to Dad by Sharon M. Kennedy

"Nightcrawlers by Ar Schneller

"Her Skin" and "Champ" by Ar Schnelle

"Heartwood" by Rebecca Tavernini

"Rewinding" and "Final Welcome" by Edzordzi Agbozo

"The Visitors" by Sarah Maurer

"Active Dreams" by Sharon Marie Brunner

Ask your local bookseller or visit www.UPReader.org to order

ISBN 978-1-61599-336-9

U.P. Reader — Issue #2

Featuring

Ask your local bookseller or visit www.UPReader.org to order

ISBN 978-1-61599-384-0